NEW ORLEANS DISASTERS

FIRSTHAND ACCOUNTS OF CRESCENT CITY TRAGEDY

ROYD ANDERSON

Published by The History Press
Charleston, SC
www.historypress.com

First published 2021

Manufactured in the United States

ISBN 9781467146364

Library of Congress Control Number: 2021945852

This book is dedicated to the victims and survivors of disasters and to all those who have helped in recovery efforts.

CONTENTS

ACKNOWLEDGEMENTS

A special thanks to Jim Davis for encouraging me to write this book and to Mary Ann Bulla for giving me sound grammatical advice.

Thank you:

Renee Allemand, Sandra Alvarez, Aida Anderson, Amanda Anderson, Eric Anderson, Dr. Mark Anderson, Sidney Anderson, Summer Anderson, Diane Anderson-Minshall, Ryan Arena, Dr. Phil Auter, John Baehr, Dr. Robert Barsley, Harold Bartholomew, Dr. John Baye, Christopher Baynas, Daniel E. Becnel Jr., Russell Bergstrom, Jennifer Boquet, Shirley Bourgeois, David Bourlet, Joseph Bourlet, Drew Broach, Kimberly Broadbridge-Navarrete, Aaron Broussard, Bob Chaisson, Charles Chatelain, Eric Coleman, Vivian Collins, Nick Congemi, Dr. Raquel Cortina, Dr. William Davie, Dr. Clayton Delery, Armond Duffourc, Tyra Duhé-Griffin, Robyn Ekings, Bill Fagaly, Skylar Fein, Lillian Francioni, Helen Freund, Lucien Gauff III, Terry Gilbert, Elaine Gonzales, Deputy Chief Frank Graff, A. Gordon Grant Jr., Laura Grenda, Lori Guin, Al Hamauei, Archbishop Philip M. Hannan, Melissa Hauck, Perez Hilton, Dr. Patricia Holmes, Fred Hurt, Jeremy Johnson, Heidi Rogers Kinchen, Tom Klekamp, Jane Kokan, Dr. Farooq Kperogi, Errol Laborde, Mark Larkin, Sheriff Harry Lee, Grace Leleux, Michael MacKenzie, Dominic Massa, Dr. Tilar J. Mazzeo, Jonathan Menard, Duane Mitchell, D.J. Mumphrey, Erin Nicole, Mary Noone, Gaynell Paradelas, Eric Paulsen, Walter Pierce, Michael Pierre, Jessica Pigott, Vickie Pigott, Evelyn

Pourciau, Allen Powell II, Emily Price, Dolores Pritchett, Tommy Pritchett, Kit Rault, Butch Remondet, Florent Retz, Peter Ricchiuti, Marcel Rivas, Gina Rivere, Brooke Robichaux, Reagan Ross, David Sandberg, Sylvia Sandberg, Elliott Sanders, Jerry Saporito, Matt Scallan, Mike Scardino, Mike Scott, Donna Silner, Chris Smith, Dr. Marcus Smith, Iris Songy, Kenneth Songy, Mary Sparacello, James Stansbury, Gregory Stassi, Ann Taylor, Roger Tilley, Johnny Townsend, Genell Turnage, John Veca, Dave Walker, Leonard A. Washofsky, Flowers Wilson, Dennis Woltering.

1

A SIGN FROM ABOVE?

The Fatima statue crying. *Illustration by Margaret Raslavich.*

It was partly cloudy and in the low seventies on the night of Monday, July 17, 1972. Father Joseph Breault made a supernatural discovery inside his Ramada Inn room at 2222 Tulane Avenue. The Pilgrim Virgin Statue was weeping! Through the evening and into the early morning, the relic sporadically shed tears over a period of four hours. During his time as the custodian of the visiting statue, this was the thirteenth and most prolonged time the padre had observed the miracle.

The remarkable Fatima cedar wood statue is one of two in the world, sculpted by José Thedim in 1947. Its appearance was ascertained through the explicit directions of Sister Lucia, who was one of the three shepherd children visited several times by Our Lady's apparition at the Cova da Iria, near the village of Fatima in Portugal in 1917.

The Ramada Inn was located five blocks from the Central Business District (CBD). In less than a year after the Pilgrim Virgin Statue wept there, three major tragedies occurred in the CBD: the Rault Center fire (November 29, 1972), the Howard Johnson's sniper (January 7, 1973) and the UpStairs Lounge fire (June 24, 1973). Incidentally, the author of this book was born during the week she wept, on Saturday, July 22, 1972.

2

THREE MAJOR TRAGEDIES IN THE CENTRAL BUSINESS DISTRICT IN LESS THAN SIX MONTHS

The Rault Center Fire (November 29, 1972)

New Orleans was strained during a disconcerting forty-five-day period in 1972.

On October 16, House Majority Leader Hale Boggs (D-LA) disappeared in Alaska and was later presumed dead. He was aboard a twin-engine Cessna 310, traveling from Anchorage to Juneau with Representative Nick Begich and his aide, Russell Brown. The plane, pilot Don Jonz and its passengers have not been located to this day. A young Bill Clinton assisted Boggs to the San Antonio airport for the first leg of the ill-fated trip.

Student protesters at Southern University had occupied the administration building on November 16 as part of a movement to restructure the university (the nation's largest Black college at the time). Unarmed freshmen Leonard Brown and Denver Smith were shot and killed during a confrontation between students, the East Baton Rouge Parish sheriff's deputies and state police. No lawman was fingered or charged with the shooting. This prompted a Black power memorial service and student boycott at Southern University in New Orleans. Most of the students didn't want to return to classes, since the Baton Rouge campus remained closed.

The week of November 26 began with a tilt. A new state law enforced on January 1 banned gambling-type pinball machines, a feat that took over forty

Hale Boggs. *Courtesy of The Historic New Orleans Collection.*

years to finally render. With 64,325 in attendance at Tulane Stadium, the Saints won only their second (and what would become their last) game of the season, defeating the Rams, 19–16. *The Godfather* was playing at the Airline and Algiers S. Drive In Theaters, while *Deliverance* was featured at the Saenger Orleans.

Mobile Oil Company geologist Michael MacKenzie has a story from this week that haunts him to this day. It occurred on the afternoon of Wednesday, November 29. He spoke of the incident from the back room office of his century-old Uptown home.

> *There's the Downtown Howard Johnson's hotel on Loyola Avenue, a block from the Rault building, and my wife Janet and I were having lunch in that hotel. When we were through lunch, we looked at each other and said, "Should we have another cup of coffee?" Which we did, and that took about fifteen more minutes. Then we walked outside the hotel onto Loyola Avenue, turned right, went about a block to the intersection of Loyola St. and Gravier St., and turned right on Gravier to get to the Rault Center. Janet was going to go up into the beauty parlor of the Rault Center and have her hair worked on. We were about twenty yards from the building when a window blew out in the front of the building, almost overhead. We stopped, because that gave us an idea that there was a fire in the building.*

Because of the window explosion, the MacKenzies did not enter the Rault Center. They stayed for about fifteen to twenty minutes longer before leaving the area, and they heard about the horrific news on later news broadcasts.

The Rault Center, located at 1111 Gravier Street, was opened on September 8, 1967, as the first New Orleans high rise to incorporate office spaces with luxury apartments. It was conceived of and owned by Joseph M. Rault Jr., a successful oilman, real estate developer, attorney and community servant. Practically half of the sixteen-story-with-penthouse skyscraper was used as office space by Mobile Oil and the Rault Petroleum Corporation. Seven floors held apartments and suites. The fifteenth floor had several meeting rooms and a beauty salon. The top floor was occupied by the exclusive Lamplighter Club, which operated a restaurant. The penthouse

Rault Center advertisement, October 22, 1967. *Courtesy of William Lanxner.*

area was used as a health club and spa, equipped with a rooftop sundeck and swimming pool.

The mysterious fire began in the Ski Chalet Meeting Room on the fifteenth floor, located roughly in the middle of the building on the Gravier Street side. The room was paneled on three sides and had a suspended ceiling with one-by-twelve-inch pine boards furred out about half an inch from one-half-inch gypsum wall board. Separated by concrete uprights, the fourth wall was composed of plate-glass windows. The floor was carpeted with a rubber underlay. Benches were secured to three of the four walls. The foam rubber–padded seats were draped with steer hides. Two panel doors adorned the wall between the Ski Chalet Room and central hall, which were about three feet apart. There were one-by-twelve-inch boards around the entryway to the Ski Chalet Room.

The undetected fire burned for an extended period, eventually gathering enough heat to blow out the quarter-inch plate-glass windows. Upon seeing this from the street below, Michael MacKenzie, who worked in the building, also saw the first puff of smoke. The fire looked as though it was fueled by natural gas. *The States-Item* quoted him as saying, "Because of the intensity of the initial flame, it reminded me of a gas flare. If you've ever been to an oil field, you know what I mean."

State Fire Marshal Raymond B. Oliver's report stated that the blaze had spread from the Ski Chalet Room into the fifteenth-floor hallway and moved in two directions, tapering toward South Rampart Street and raging toward Loyola Avenue, where it reached the Lamplighter Beauty Salon, which was catty-corner from the Ski Chalet Room.

Inside the salon, Jannas McBeth, Wilma Williams, Natalie Smith, Norris Farley and Jacqueline Maillho heard the fire, saw smoke and rushed to a corner window. There was little to stifle or stop the fire that was spreading

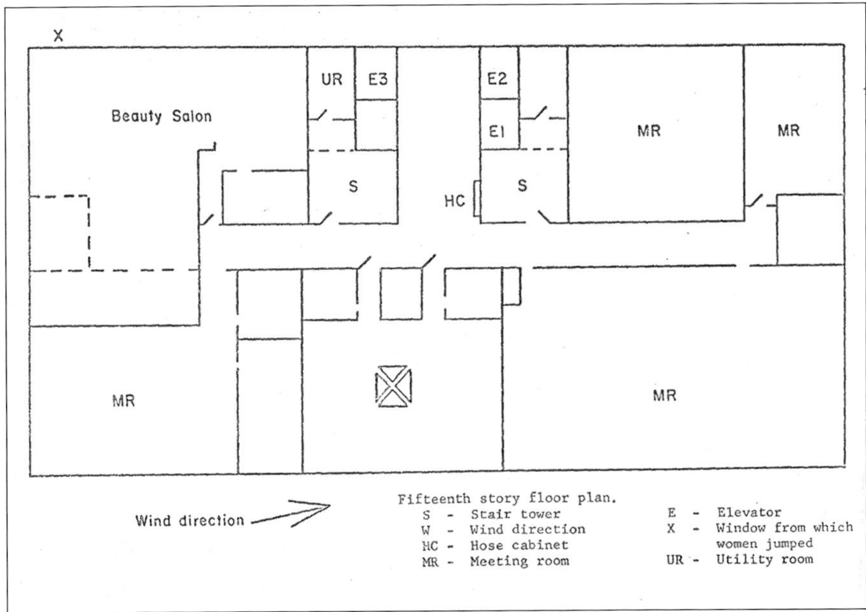

Fifteenth-floor blueprint. *Courtesy of the NFPA.*

toward the women, since the door between the hallway and salon entrance was typically left open. Flanked by the asphyxiating smoke, McBeth broke the window with a shampoo chair.

The idiom "which way the wind blows" is a metaphor for a course of events. In the case of the Rault Center fire, the wind was a villain. As a result of McBeth smashing out the window, the wind, blowing past that corner of the building, generated an area of low pressure, drawing the heat and smoke toward the women. A draft was also blowing in from the broken windows of the Ski Chalet Room, creating a high-pressure area on that side of the building. This also helped spread the fire in the interior toward the salon.

Six air miles away, Dr. Raquel Cortina, in her first year as an Assistant Professor of Applied Music and Opera at the University of New Orleans, looked out of her studio window in the newly constructed Performing Arts Center; the scary sight of the city skyline is still etched in her memory: "I saw these flames just flickering a little bit, and I still went and started working with my student and the pianist. Then, I turned around to go back to my desk, and I see these flames just growing and growing! It was just really, really bad."

At 1:28 p.m., the New Orleans Fire Department (NOFD) got its first call. The switchboard lit up "like a Christmas tree," according to the dispatcher.

Dr. Raquel Cortina beside the same UNO studio window that she peered through in 1972 to view the Rault Center Fire. *Author's collection.*

In a brief period, more than one hundred calls about the fire were received. The calls came from outside the Rault Center, and all said the flames were coming from the upper floors. The fire ascended the side of the building and went into the windows of the Lamplighter Club on the sixteenth floor.

The first fire engine arrived at the scene at 1:30 p.m. Upon seeing the enormity of the blaze, a second alarm was raised. Two minutes later, reports of people trapped in the building were received, and a third alarm was promptly called. Firemen went to the rooftop of the neighboring Saratoga Building's garage at the rear of the Rault Center, and phone calls to the department said there were people trapped at the fifteenth-story rear window. The women were located by the fire brigade at 1:35 p.m. From the garage roof, they attempted the rescue with a fifty-five-foot-tall ladder, but it only reached to the thirteenth floor, two stories below the women. Many failed attempts were made with a rope gun to shoot a rope into the window where the women were trapped. Each try required the rope to be rewound, a slow process that took away precious minutes. Why did the New Orleans Fire Department have only one rope gun at such a disastrous scene?

A crowd of onlookers amassed on Common Street and the neutral ground on Loyola Avenue; many were on their lunch hour or were

The Rault Center burning. *Courtesy of The Historic New Orleans Collection.*

Christmas shopping. The squeaking of brakes, car horns, roaring mufflers and rattling suspension systems faded from the atmosphere as a police motorcycle patrol closed off traffic. The frantic ladies above waved handkerchiefs and shouted to the firemen and cops below, their cries suppressed by the raging firestorm. By then, fifteen minutes had passed, and time was running out.

At the Lamplighter Club, a reward ceremony was taking place for employee Luis Suazo. Approximately 100 to 150 people were gathered there, including Joe Rault. Ironically, he was awarding Suazo one hundred dollars for discovering and extinguishing a fire that had been reported to the New Orleans Fire Department at 7:59 a.m. that morning. The fire had occurred on the sixteenth floor on the opposite side of the building. When Suazo

Ladder too short. *Courtesy of* The Times-Picayune.

discovered it, thick, black smoke was gushing out of a small room's closed doorway. There were fires in two areas of the room. It makes one wonder about the probability of two fires in one day and the possibility of arson. The building tenants might have misjudged the pungent smell of smoke for recurring smoke stench from the morning fire, stalling early detection of the afternoon fire.

When patrons of the Lamplighter Club saw flames out of the windows and many heard the sound of an explosion, they rushed to the nearest stairwell. One man, as he was running down the stairs, thought he heard a knocking sound at the fifteenth floor. Thinking this may have been a person trying to escape to the stairwell, he opened the door. He saw nothing but flames and shut the door. Evidently, the noise he heard was the expanding of the door in its metal frame. Warped by the heat, the door did not shut completely. Heat and smoke poured into the stairwell, and eight men were forced to make an alternate escape route by climbing a drainage pipe to the roof.

A few floors below the fire, a civilian rescue attempt was underway. Twenty-six-year-old William J. Allen, twenty-six-year-old Lloyd Caldwell, thirty-six-year-old Charles J. Michel Sr. and an unidentified man took the elevator to assist. Allen and Caldwell were New Orleans Public Service Inc. (NOPSI) employees who had just checked the building's gas service after the morning fire. Michel was an elevator repairman who was working in the building. As they approached the floor that contained the fire, the unidentified man panicked. He stopped the elevator and got off several floors below the fire, while the remaining three good Samaritans continued the rescue mission. When the fifteenth-floor elevator doors opened, a burst of flames and hot gases knocked the men to the floor. Michel lost consciousness and lay face up.

Meanwhile, firefighters from the Flying Squad bolted up the stairwell for an interior attack, but they had difficulty getting into the fifteenth floor, due to the copious fire and smoke. When they finally reached the fifteenth floor, they knocked down the flames and were soon joined by four other crews. Firefighters rescued Allen and Caldwell, who were able to survive by lying face down. Sadly, Michel was already deceased; he had died from smoke inhalation. Allen and the critically injured Caldwell were removed to the fourteenth floor and administered first aid. A fireman carried Michel's body and placed it on a chair in the stairwell landing between the eighth and ninth floors.

Three firefighter crews on the fifteenth floor attempted to free the women from the flash fire, its ever-increasing strength nourished by salon products and aerosol cans. Using one-and-a-half-inch hose lines from the standpipes in the stair tower, their rate of water application was inadequate with the occasional low pressure. The lines were previously cut by falling glass outside of the building. At one point during the rescue attempt, only a partition (one layer of gypsum wall board) separated the firemen from the women, unbeknownst to the firefighters. In WWL-TV news photographer Peter Lambousy's video that was shot live at the scene, manager and beautician Jannas McBeth, thirty, can be seen from the window, screaming down below to the masses while pointing to her right, "The fireman's right there!" Did McBeth hear how close he was?

A team of firefighters was on the floor below the beauty salon. Their mission was to break out windows and send ladders up one story. No visual evidence or fire investigation documents indicate that ladders were sent up from their standpoint, the fourteenth floor. A broken window directly below four of the ladies was visible in press photographs on the scene.

In the dreary, wintry sky above, two private helicopters voluntarily called themselves into action to save those trapped on the burning roof. The first copter on the scene was piloted by John F. Lockwood of Offshore Helicopters in Houma. Lockwood was a former aviator for the Royal Air Force and had only been in the United States for a year. In an attempt to clear a path for the chopper, the men who were in peril tore down a television antenna, impeding his landing. Lockwood rescued six men in two trips, dropping them off on the lawn of City Hall. Two remained on the unstable and fiery summit of the Rault Center.

Captain Albert Carriger of Metairie was charting a path in his helicopter for an upcoming Jefferson Parish Santa Claus Parade when the radio tower at the New Orleans International Airport sent word for help. In a death-

A lady prays in front of the BNO Building. *Courtesy of The Historic New Orleans Collection.*

defying moment, he swept over the Rault Center roof and scooped up the two men at 1:49 p.m. He was hovering so close that the copter's tail rotor caught fire. Soon afterward, the roof collapsed.

The third helicopter on the scene was piloted by Joseph Davis, a commander of the flight division of the Jefferson Parish Sheriff's Office. Sergeant Joseph Livaudais was also aboard, serving as the observer. Using a public address system, Davis warned people on neighboring rooftops to vacate. Dangerous particles from the fire were sailing through the sky.

For nearly a half hour, the women trapped at the beauty salon window pleaded for help. The crowd, press and first responders below begged them not to jump.

Twenty-six-year-old salon employee Wilma Williams kept wanting to jump to escape the flames. Manager and beautician McBeth took a leadership role in the torrid parlor, trying to keep Williams and the ladies calm. According to the National Fire Protection Association (NFPA) report, the helicopter crew tried to drop a line to them. Unfortunately, the air currents around the building prevented the small helicopter from getting close enough. The wind was the antagonist once again.

A private citizen called the Coast Guard for help. At 1:51 p.m., the Coast Guard radioed that it was converging on the scene with a large helicopter and would attempt to rescue the women with their drop lines. A minute later, the firefighters on the Saratoga Building garage roof below the women announced that one of the ladies was hanging out of the infernal window. Williams was clinging on for dear life with only her right hand, which was grasping the hand of McBeth; she was extending down and kicking the window beneath them. As she courageously tried to break the plate glass and create an escape route to the unscathed floor below, Williams seemed to be losing her grip. To compensate, she raised her left arm and grabbed the foot of thirty-one-year-old and seven-months-pregnant Jacqueline Maillho, her stocking-covered legs dangling above Williams outside the salon window. With orange flames and black smoke encroaching, Maillho struggled in a seated position at the edge of the windowsill. Williams lost her grip and fell eight stories to the garage roof of the Saratoga Building. People below shrieked and turned away in horror as the valiant Black lady in a yellow dress left their eyesight, but she never left their subconsciouses.

The fire was blazing out the salon window when fifty-six-year-old Norris Farley, a legal secretary, leapt shortly after Williams. Eyewitness Wayne Williams said it looked like she was on fire. Her body tumbled down the side of the building, hitting it multiple times fiercely. Onlookers screamed.

The smoke and flames then bellowed out of the salon, making it look like a dragon's lair. McBeth, dressed in a red short-sleeved blouse, dark skirt and hosiery, was suspended outside, hanging onto the window rail with both hands. Natalie Smith, thirty-nine, was to her right at this moment, her back facing McBeth. Smith was leaning forward over the ledge and holding the window rail with her left hand. Her left foot was planted on the windowsill. Swinging her right leg over, she presumably attempted to toe hook the corner of the building with her knee-high boot and missed. Being the only lady to keep her footwear on, she also held onto a green alligator purse and mink coat in her right hand. Smith may also have been trying to get to the rooftop of the Loyola building (its official name was the DeMontluzin Building), which would have taken a world-record-long jump at an impossible angle. As her body projected back toward the fumes, McBeth unselfishly released her right hand from the window rail and dropped her arm to her side, giving Smith the space she needed to land securely on the ledge. A little less than a second later, McBeth's left hand slipped from the frame. In a feat of great agility, as she was falling, she clutched the legs of Maillho in front of her as a last attempt at survival. Her right hand quickly slid off, then her left. A monstrous burst of smoke emerged from the window. From the lens of Lambousy, McBeth's silhouette was seen holding a purse in her right hand as she descended to the garage roof. About four seconds later, Smith fell and tumbled head first toward an apparent instant death. In quick succession, Maillho, while climbing to the window below her, lost her balance and plummeted from the building about six seconds after Smith. Four seconds later, a loud, cannon-like explosion of black smoke from the salon floor pierced the ears of the watchers below.

At 1:53 p.m., a radio dispatch from the garage roof of the Saratoga Building said all five women had fallen eight stories to the roof in a period of roughly thirty seconds. In Lambousy's video, a cop, fireman and civilian can be seen carrying Williams from the rooftop. The portion of her left leg below the knee is dangling, nearly severed. The scene makes Joe Theismann's 1985 leg break by Lawrence Taylor on *Monday Night Football* look tame.

A fifth alarm crew from the NOFD rolled in at 1:55 p.m. Two Coast Guard helicopters arrived at the scene six minutes too late, at 1:59 p.m., followed by an Army chopper. The attempts to rescue the women had failed. The blaze was reported to be under control at 3:14 p.m. Helping the firemen extinguish the last shimmer of the deadly fire, a heavy rain began to fall around 4:00 p.m. The winter skies darkened as the temperature dropped even more. Superfluous sorrow and eeriness set in.

Six people died as a result of the Rault Center fire. Jannas McBeth, Jacqueline Maillho, her unborn child of seven months, Norris Farley and Charles J. Michel Sr. died at the scene. Wilma Williams remained unconscious and in critical condition with multiple fractures to her arms and legs and head injuries until her death at Charity Hospital on December 23, 1972. Lloyd Caldwell later succumbed to his burn injuries and smoke inhalation on January 10, 1973, at Southern Baptist Hospital. The death rate for the fire was low; over four hundred people evacuated the building safely.

When Natalie Smith fell from the window and struck the garage roof, like Wilma Williams, she also landed on her feet, having traveled thirty-two yards in three seconds. Smith crushed an ankle and broke both legs, her back, ribs, pelvis, collarbone and teeth. Doctors theorized that due to the girdle she always wore, she sustained no internal injuries. After being in a coma at Charity Hospital for nearly two months, Smith awoke to the voice of her son, Marcel Rivas, who was prodding her to take her liquid nourishment.

Smith's husband, Roy, a paraplegic, used a wheelchair as a result of a 1961 diving accident in the Gulf of Mexico. He was pulled up too quickly, causing nitrogen bubbles to form in his body. In the 1960s, Natalie and Roy wanted to publish a magazine for the handicapped. Now, in a cruel ironic twist, both were afflicted with horrific, debilitating accidents that affected their lives. Due to the Rault Center fire, Natalie's faith took a turn, and she switched from Lutheran to Baptist. She lived with aches and pains; one of her legs was two inches shorter than the other, and she wore special shoes when necessary. Through the years, she told her motivational, faith-driven story of survival and recovery to many, even once appearing as a special guest on *The Oprah Winfrey Show*. Winfrey's guests were always given first-class treatment, spending an overnight evening in her luxury penthouse that overlooked the Chicago skyline. Still haunted by the Rault Center fire, Natalie's phobia of high-rises kept her from that experience. Being an accommodating, generous and kind host, Winfrey had the entire second floor of her building renovated and prepared for Natalie.

From her lovely, eight-acre home, nestled in the rolling hills of Tylertown, Mississippi, Genell Turnage reflected back on her sister, Jannas McBeth:

> *I was five and a half years older than she was, and of course, back then, they didn't talk about pregnancies and babies and how they came, so I saved enough dimes to buy my little sister. I saved for several years, and finally, almost six years later, I had enough money to buy me a little sister, and that sister was Gene. She was very special.*

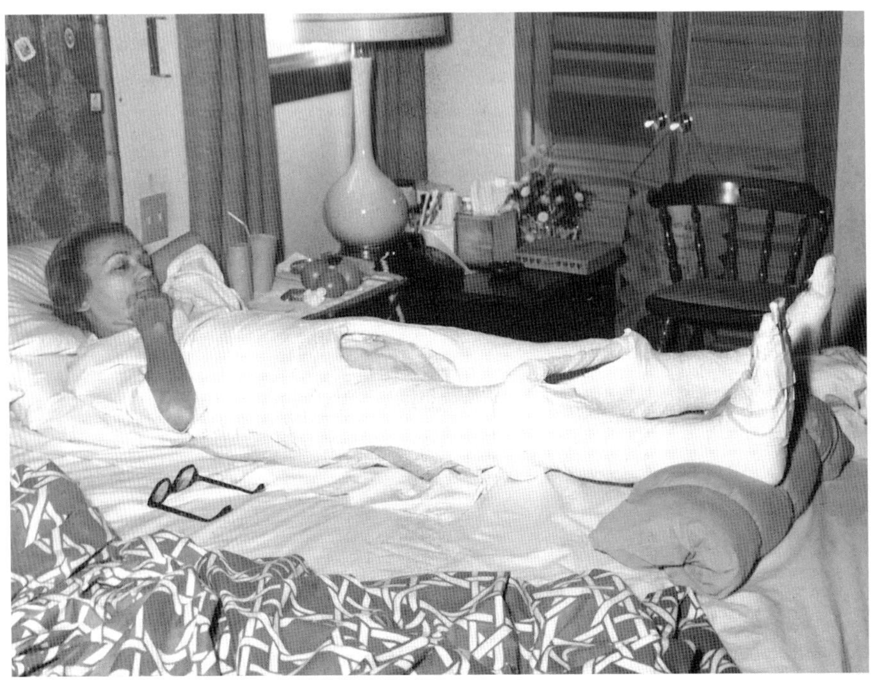

Natalie Smith's grueling recovery. *Courtesy of Vickie Pigott.*

> *Her name was Jannas Geneva McBeth, but everyone called her Gene. She loved music. She loved to sing. She could play the guitar, bass guitar, accordion, piano and organ. We had a lot of sing-alongs with the children and even the adults in the family. She'd play the guitar, and I'd play the piano. She was so talented. She thoroughly enjoyed doing ladies' hair and making them beautiful. Most of her customers would say that she had magic in her hands.*
>
> *Gene had a son: Victor. He was fifteen years old in 1972. He followed in her footsteps; he was a hairdresser also. He was talented, a lot like his mom. Victor passed away in 2008 of cancer. He was a young man—always remembered his mom and always missed her.*

November 29, 1972, is very hard for her to talk about. She said:

> *My husband, myself and two of my children were in McComb, Mississippi, shopping that afternoon. The store we were in had a radio on, and the radio said there's been a fire in the Rault Center in New Orleans. We hopped in the car, and my husband drove one hundred miles per hour, and more part*

Natalie Smith on *The Oprah Winfrey Show*. *Courtesy of Vickie Pigott.*

of the time, until we got to New Orleans. Of course, it was dark by the time we got there, but we kept trying to find out where she was. We went to hospitals, and we finally learned she was at the mortuary. My husband went in and identified the body there. And so much of that is a blur to me. I know it was so hard for my mom to learn that.

Later, we saw television pictures of it actually happening, and almost every year, for a long, long time, on the anniversary date, they showed it on TV. We tried to keep my mother from seeing it each time, but sometimes, it was unavoidable, and that was very hard.

The Rault Center fire was arguably the most dramatic fire in New Orleans history. Watching the women falling to their deaths on TV news broadcasts was a trauma that became ingrained in the psyche of many. Michael MacKenzie, who witnessed the inception of the fire while walking down Gravier Street, saw the aftermath on the news. Had he and his wife, Janet, not had another cup of coffee at the Howard Johnson's hotel that afternoon, her fate would've been quite different. The cerebral geologist remarked: "You hear stories sort of like this—how close people come to

Multitalented Gene McBeth. *Courtesy of Genell Turnage.*

dying—but you never think you're going to be one of those stories. In my wife's case, she was! Janet, going to the place where so many women were killed, was about maybe five to ten minutes away from being in that number. We loved coffee from then on."

Debates arose about why the firefighters didn't use a life net to catch the women. The New Orleans Fire Department defended its position using physics. Falling eight stories, a 160-pound person's impact force would be 12,960 pounds due to kinetic energy. The net would've split. The women landed on the roof ten to thirty feet apart. Using the suggested eight men required to hold the net, they would have had only 2.25 seconds to move the net under each falling body. This feat would have been virtually impossible, according to the NFPA.

What caused the two fires at the Rault Center? To this day, no one has a solid answer. State Fire Marshal Raymond B. Oliver definitely thought it was arson and that both fires were linked. He speculated, "It is reasonable to assume they came back in the afternoon to do what they didn't do earlier."

Tests by Shilstone Laboratories revealed that there were petroleum products in the location of the fire. Oliver said it had not been determined what exactly the cans contained, but it was either gasoline, kerosene, naphtha or some other petroleum product.

The fire investigation included interviews with over two hundred people, and thirty-five successfully took lie detector tests. One of those who passed was a man who supposedly warned a woman in the Rault Center to "get out of the building" before the afternoon fire started. Police cleared him of any connection with the fire.

Joe Rault agreed with Oliver's assertions and spoke publicly about the tragedy shortly after the Howard Johnson's sniper incident, which occurred a block away thirty-nine days later, on January 7, 1973. After seeing a photograph of the sniper, Mark Essex, a Rault Center security guard who was on duty the day of the fire remembered two sharply dressed, suspicious men in the lobby that morning, one matching Essex's description. They read the directory and went up the elevator. Later, they were seen back in the lobby. Rault also commented on the similarities between the fires at the Rault Center and Howard Johnson's sniper incident: "Whatever accelerant was used in our fire—kerosene, petroleum or otherwise—just gave it that explosive effect. It was almost instantaneous. It was very similar to the way the fires in the Howard Johnson's exploded out."

Some theorized Essex burned the roof of the Rault Center in order to prevent police sharpshooters from being able to perch from it during his rooftop rampage.

Alerting the public of this new twist in the investigation, Rault partnered with *The Times-Picayune* in offering a $25,000 reward leading to the arrest of the person or persons responsible for the fire. This hefty sum in 1973 standards has yet to be collected.

Another prevailing conspiracy theory about the cause of the fire is Rault's membership in Truth and Consequences of New Orleans Inc., an alliance of fifty businessmen who were financing District Attorney Jim Garrison's investigation into the John F. Kennedy assassination. Was someone trying to rub Rault out?

Though the building itself was fire resistive, no sprinkler system had been installed. Additionally, the Lamplighter Club restaurant ceiling was combustible. The Rault Center was built in compliance with the safety standards of the New Orleans Building Code. Sprinkler systems and outside fire escapes were not required for buildings with a concrete frame. The code did not include any regulations for decorations, furnishings or other contents that may raise fire hazards. The duplicity of the code initiated a movement to make a change. Affirmed by the deaths of nine elderly residents in a fire at the newly constructed, eleven-story Baptist Towers in Atlanta the morning after the Rault Center fire, the perfunctory statute rose to widespread

An aerial view showing the proximity between the Rault Center and the Downtown Howard Johnson's hotel—two major tragedies thirty-nine days apart. *Courtesy of* The Times-Picayune.

concern. In 1974, major strides for fire safety legislation were made, driven by New Orleans Fire Department Superintendent William McCrossen and Representative Charles Grisbaum. Louisiana became the first state in the nation to require automatic sprinkler systems in all high-rise buildings constructed after 1975. This law was strengthened in a local ordinance passed by the New Orleans City Council the same year.

Entrepreneur John Scurlock, a plastics guru from Metairie who worked for NASA and taught at Tulane University, invented the Space Walk Safety Air Cushion shortly after sprinkler systems were penned into state law. Inspired by witnessing the forlorn results of the Rault Center tragedy, Scurlock presented the self-inflating air mattress as a gift to the New Orleans Fire Department on June 4, 1974. The cushion can safely catch persons who are forced to jump from as high as twelve stories; it absorbs the weight of their bodies, softening their impact. When inflated, the fireproof nylon–vinyl coating life pack is eighteen by twenty-five feet around and eight and a half feet deep. It takes about a minute to inflate, weighs approximately 285

The Space Walk Safety Air Cushion, 1980. *Courtesy of David K. Persons.*

pounds and can be put into place by two people. The Space Walk Safety Air Cushion is now a staple in fire departments across the globe. The mattress is also beloved among Hollywood stunt men.

From his 1959 invention of the inflatable amusement ride known as the Space Walk (now commonly referred to as a bounce house) to being the brainchild of the Space Walk Safety Air Cushion, Scurlock's ingenuity has transfixed generations.

The majority of lawsuits involving the Rault Center fire were settled out of court by Joe Rault and his insurers in April 1975. The payout amounts were never published. Mentioned but absolved from the settlements were the City of New Orleans and then–Fire Superintendent Louis San Salvador. Court records reveal that the federal and state suits filed were "compromised," which typically means the plaintiffs got less than they asked for. The suits that were seeking more than $35 million were part of the out-of-court settlements filed by the families of Jannas McBeth, Natalie Smith, Wilma Williams and others. Joe Rault sued the Continental Insurance Company for failing to live

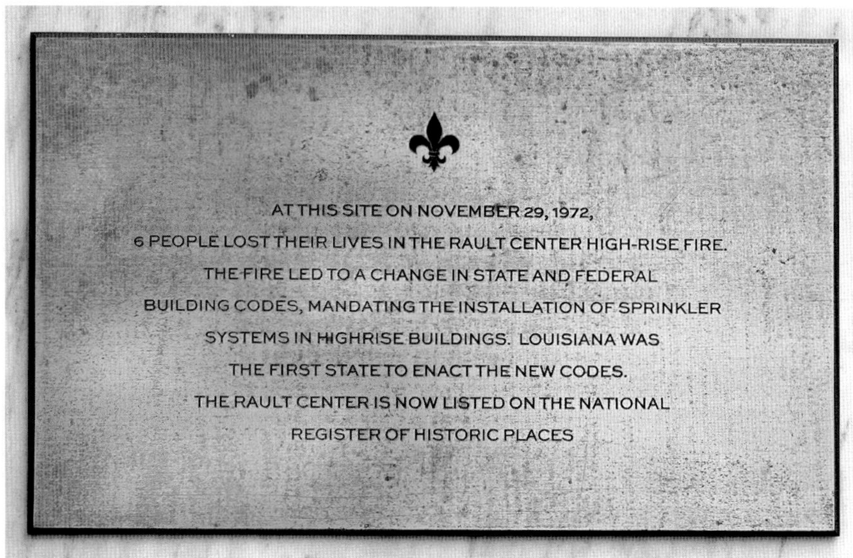

Above: The Rault Center Fire plaque at the entrance of the Troubadour Hotel. *Courtesy of Melissa Hauck.*

Left: A view of the Rault Center building from Common Street, 2021. Notice the infamous window is now sealed. The ladies fell onto the Saratoga Building garage rooftop (*bottom left*). *Courtesy of Melissa Hauck.*

up to the agreements in the building's coverage; a settlement out of court was reached in August 1975.

The Rault Center stood closed for a year and a half after the fire, undergoing renovations to be converted into the Rault Hotel. On the morning of February 8, 1974, thirty-one-year-old electrician Karl Schega fell to his death from the building's thirteenth-floor linen chute to the fourth floor. The dark and muddy gray aura that surrounded the edifice once again turned black, consuming another soul. In 1975, the Rault Hotel became the Holiday Inn Superdome. During the 1980s, it was converted into apartments and timeshare properties. The building was up for auction in 1984, 1986 and 1988.

Sidney Anderson, a NOPSI residential representative who witnessed the Rault Center's exploding windows and falling glass and the arrival of the West Bank's David Crockett fire truck during his 2:00 p.m. lunch break that tragic afternoon in 1972, was also present at one of the auctions of the building in the 1980s. This auction was held at the Howard Johnson's hotel across the street. Anderson was an account representative for NOPSI at that time. He reflected on the event:

> *It was real fancy. They had a fellow playing the piano, cocktails, waitresses handing out hors d'oeuvres. The opening bid was around $800,000. I remember the auctioneer saying, "Okay, we've got this great, sturdy building!" I was thinking in my head, "Yeah, it's a sturdy building, but it doesn't have any electricity—they don't have a switchboard!" He couldn't get an opening bid. So, that was the end of it. That auction lasted about ten minutes. It was kind of sad for Mr. Rault. I enjoyed working with Mr. Rault. He was a nice guy and easy to do business with.*

On January 20, 2015, the Rault Center at 1111 Gravier Street was added to the National Register of Historic Places. In 2017, the building got a second chance at life and became the Troubadour Hotel. A plaque in memory of the victims of the Rault Center fire is erected outside the entrance door.

The Howard Johnson's Sniper (January 7, 1973)

At President Richard Nixon's second inaugural address on January 20, 1973, an additional six hundred agents were there to protect the incumbent, who won in a landslide (Massachusetts prevented a fifty-state sweep). Why did they need the reinforcements, since he just broke the record for the widest popular vote margin in any post–World War II U.S. presidential election? Thirteen days earlier, a twenty-three-year-old former Navy dental technician, who was enrolled in a New Orleans vending machine repair school and at the top of his class, dispensed terror in the Crescent City. The polite Dryades Street tenant, who complimented his neighbor's morning prayers, brought fear to the nation's forefront one cold, miserable Sunday.

It was the Tuesday after New Year's, January 2, 1973. A young, goateed Black man wearing an Army fatigue jacket and cargo pants walked out of the cold and into Joe's Grocery Store in Gert Town at closing time. Shuffling to the counter, the stranger asked the proprietor, Joe Perniciaro, to get the Schick Championship razor on the shelf for him; it was a promotional 1972 Olympics blade with a red-white-and-blue stripe on its milky-colored handle. Only four months earlier, eleven members of the Israeli Olympic team had been massacred by the Palestinian Black September organization at the Munich Games.

As the drifter left Joe's with his purchase and traversed toward Earhart Boulevard, Perniciaro noticed the man was concealing his bloody, bandaged, left hand inside his jacket pocket. Police had made it known that they were on the lookout for someone who fit that description. An hour after closing the store, Perniciaro, along with his fourteen-year-old stock clerk, Darryl Davis, went to the Criminal Investigation Department and reported their encounter to Detective Emmett Dupas. Did the storekeeper and kid just meet the most wanted man in New Orleans?

A couple of nights earlier, on New Year's Eve, a sniper had shot three police officers in two separate locations. Alfred Harrell, nineteen, recently married with a nine-month-old boy and a stellar Loyola University criminology student, was shot and killed at 10:55 p.m. in the driveway of Central Lockup with a .44-caliber Magnum bullet. Lieutenant Horace Perez was wounded in the ambush, hit in the foot and leg. Rounds were discovered in two areas of a vacant lot that were 264 and 464 feet away, near the I-10, which was being built at the time.

The combat-booted killer ran for cover to an industrial hideaway, the Burkhart Manufacturing Company warehouse on 1065 South Gayoso Street. Unknown to him, he dropped a brown leather bag with an ominous black owl's face painted on it on a service road. The hit kit contained two cans of lighter fluid, a sixty-five-foot-long roll of bell wire and six live .44-caliber Magnum cartridges. Gaining access to the warehouse through an open window, the sniper gashed his hand. Blood trickled everywhere inside the shivering repository as the ADT silent alarm system was triggered.

A patrol car soon approached the warehouse, its red-and-blue lights flashing. The sniper's adrenaline escalated as he positioned himself behind a desk in front of a window, taking aim at the vehicle with his rifle from the shrouded shadows. Sergeant Ed Hosli, a young K-9 officer with four children and a wife; rookie officer Harold Blappert; and Hosli's dog, Ike, had arrived at what seemed to be a routine false alarm call. As Hosli turned back to the car to release Ike, two shots rang out; the sergeant collapsed, shot twice in the back and seriously wounded.

The assassin managed to escape once again and sprinted six blocks to find shelter in a little white and weathered wooden Baptist church on 1208 South Lopez Street. Along the way, he dropped a forensic trail of ten rounds of .44 Magnum cartridges and blood droplets from his wound.

Reverend Sylvester Williams went to the chapel at 6:00 p.m. the following evening, January 1, to make preparations for the 8:00 p.m. service. With his key in hand, he noticed the worn front door had been forced open. Trembling as he entered, Williams spotted a Black man in the rear of the church. The pastor quickly left, reporting the intruder to the police. When the cops arrived, the trespasser was gone.

At 7:30 p.m. on January 3, an anonymous caller tipped off law enforcement; the man was again hiding in the church. Once again, the lethal escape artist was nowhere to be seen when the police arrived. Police did discover bloodstains on the benches and walls, a bag of .38-caliber cartridges hidden in the bathroom and a handwritten note addressed to the minister, apologizing for the break-in. Did the sniper have a salutary spiritual experience? Had he conquered the evil that had taken possession of him?

The resounding answer arrived on the Lord's Day, Sunday, January 7, 1973. Entering Joe's Grocery that morning on a mission, he quickly located Joe Perniciaro and yelled, "You, come here!"

The startled grocer looked up. *BANG*! He was shot in the neck with a .44-caliber round; Perniciaro would survive the assault, undergoing months of rehabilitation. The intuitive gunman was apparently seeking revenge on the informant he had bought a razor from five nights earlier.

Fleeing the scene, he darted down the 1500 block of South White Street and carjacked Marvin Albert at 10:40 a.m. from the front seat of his 1968 black-over-beige Chevelle. Police soon gave chase as the rifleman stormed toward Downtown, colliding with a vehicle on Washington Avenue and Dupre Street. The stunned but alert driver jotted the hit-and-run culprit's license plate number down. Guessing incorrectly at a fork in the road, the patrolman who was in pursuit punched the accelerator toward the Calliope project. The directors of the then-popular *Adam-12* TV show couldn't have choreographed a more suspenseful chase; the suspect had escaped in cinematic fashion.

As the driver approached the Downtown Howard Johnson's hotel parking garage like a bat out of hell, the parking attendant yelled at him to slow down. The young Black man sped by him up the ramp to the fourth floor, where he slammed the Chevelle into park at the nearest spot and shut off the motor. It was then 11:00 a.m.; the twenty-eight-hour nightmare had begun.

Heavy, rubber-soled combat boots charged to the zone of action: the stairwell. Yanking at locked metal doorknobs on each level, the shooter finally gained access to the hotel's eighteenth floor. Armed with a rifle and running down the carpeted hallway toward three Black employees congregated near a linen cart, he suddenly stopped and stared. The vivacissimo tempo of the gunman's pulse was then in unison with the maids. "Don't worry, I'm not going to shoot you Black people. I want the Whites," he said.

Continuing down the corridor, headed for the elevators, the man encountered Dr. Robert Steagall, a Virginian honeymooning in New Orleans with his wife, Betty. A struggle ensued outside of their room, 1829, as the young doctor attempted to disarm the miscreant, who raised the rifle at him. Steagall valiantly grabbed him by the waist and lifted him off the ground, raring for a two-point takedown. The gunman swung his rifle like an axe, pummeling Steagall's collarbone. The rattled physician hit the floor and scrambled to get up; two shots exploded from the barrel. The twenty-eight-year-old newlywed was dead, shot in the chest and arm.

Betty's deafening shrill startled the killer as she rushed from the room at him. "Is this really happening?" she thought. Only yesterday, a postcard was placed in the mail to Robert's mother, exalting this unique city and the fun it offers. As the shooter shoved Betty away, the shrieking intensified as she knelt beside Robert, cradling his head. The cold-blooded killer shot her execution style in the back of the head; the honeymooners died in a final embrace.

Entering their room, he grabbed the telephone book, placed it underneath a curtain and lit it on fire. Eight diversionary fires were started in the hotel in that manner on floors eight, eleven, sixteen, seventeen and eighteen. When Frank Schneider, fifty-two, the hotel's assistant manager, was informed of the horror above by the maids, he bravely went to investigate. The murderer encountered him on the eleventh floor; a shot

Watercolor painting of the Downtown Howard Johnson's hotel by Jeannette Boutall Woest, 1968. *Courtesy of The Historic New Orleans Collection.*

from his .44 Magnum rifle shattered the back of Schneider's skull as he attempted to flee down the stairwell.

Counting the minutes since Schneider had left, hotel manager Walter Collins grew concerned and decided to check on him. He ran into the gunman on the tenth floor. Slouched over in the stairwell with a .44 Magnum slug in his stomach, Collins would die eight days later, on January 15, 1973, in his wife's arms in Charity Hospital.

With the sounds of cannons blasting, billowing smoke and crackling fire, a young Black maid perspired profusely, hidden inside a room. She was soon to be discovered by the gunman. She asserted: "He pointed that big gun at me and laughed. All of a sudden, a White man came out of the next room and got between me and the man with the gun—like to protect me. Well, when the dude saw that, he told the White boy, 'Fella—you just saved your life, and you saved that Black chick's life, too.' And then he ran up the stairs, fast—very fast."

One of the many diversionary fires set. The sniper, highly intelligent and skilled in guerrilla warfare, also threw diversionary firecrackers, startling the police and enhancing chaos. *Courtesy of* The Times-Picayune.

First responders were pressed into action, surrounding the building's perimeter. NOFD truckies cussed as Lieutenant Tim Ursin fell from his ladder, shot in the arm. Police sharpshooters positioned themselves on the top floors and roofs of nearby buildings, including the Rault Center; its partial skeletal remains still evident. Standing in front of an open ninth-floor window of the Loyola building, patrolman Charley Arnold was shot in the face, the left side of his jaw pulverized. The round had come from the smoke-filled patio of the Howard Johnson's hotel, near the swimming pool. Arnold survived this attack.

A command post was set up by New Orleans Police Department (NOPD) Superintendent Clarence Giarrusso on the ground level of the hotel. Mayor Moon Landrieu soon joined him as an advisor. Chomping his cigar, the bureaucrat brainstormed ideas on how to exit the Seventh Circle of Hell before them. Over six hundred police officers were called into duty, including deputies from neighboring parishes, state troopers, cops from Mississippi

Left: Fireman shot. *Courtesy of* The Times-Picayune.

Below: NOPD sharpshooter. *Courtesy of* The Times-Picayune.

and Texas, FBI and Treasury agents and other federal agents. The press was on the front line as well, their cameras used as cudgels of authenticity for the terror-stricken viewers at home. Unfortunately, Giarrusso's command post neglected the power of broadcast journalism. Relying on word-of-mouth communication and out-of-focus photographs, a portable TV would have helped their strategics tremendously.

Duncan Plaza, a grassy knoll overlooking the front of the Howard Johnson's hotel, was crawling with policemen. Sergeant Pal Palmisano wailed and hit the ground near car 130; a sniper bullet had ripped through his left shoulder. Father Peter V. Rogers, chaplain of the NOFD and NOPD, assisted ambulance driver Chris Caton in securing him to a stretcher. Bullets sprayed. The priest's faith was his shield. He stated:

> *I was picking up my sick call kit from the ground when a dull, sickening thud dug into the grass not more than three feet away from me. It was a .44 Magnum slug that missed. I yanked open the front door of the ambulance and literally drove into the seat. I glanced back to the left. My blood froze at what I saw. Lying close to a large tree, about twenty feet away, was a young policeman. The glazed look of death already masked his face. Officer Ken Solis, also badly wounded, was attempting to crawl over to help his comrade. The wounded cop put his bloodied hand on the man's chest, then dropped his head in grief and hopelessness.*

The padre held on to Palmisano's stretcher as Caton peeled out with the back doors open. The medic morphed into a patient, wounded by a sniper bullet in the left shoulder blade, then had the stretcher roll over his fingers inside the cabin. At the Charity Hospital Emergency Room, Father Rogers administered the last rites for twenty-six-year-old Officer Phil Coleman. He had a wife and little boy.

Patrolman Paul Persigo, thirty-three, parked his police car in the middle of the street and got behind it for cover. Firemen and bystanders joined him. The sniper waited. A man suddenly ran toward them. Persigo rose and warned him of the gunman; shot in the mouth with a .44 Magnum bullet, the patrolman was instantly killed. Persigo died helping a stranger. He was survived by his wife, Judy, and three young children: Mark, ten; Steven, eight; and Holly, three.

The severity of the situation intensified at 1:00 p.m., when NOPD Deputy Superintendent Louis Sirgo led a rescue party of five policemen for Mike Burl and Bob Childress, the two cops who were trapped inside the hotel's smoke-filled elevator on the eighteenth floor. Sirgo was the epitome

Patrolman Leo Newman takes the pulse of mortally wounded patrolman Phil Coleman. Wounded Eighth District NOPD Officer Ken Solis leans his head against a tree. *Courtesy of* The Times-Picayune.

of a tough, crewcut veteran cop, starring in the 1958 movie *New Orleans After Dark*. Their stealthy, south stairwell ascent was interrupted by a deafening detonation from above. "I'm dying—my Jesus, I'm dying!"

Sirgo screamed his last words, collapsing on the dingy fifteenth-floor landing with a severed spine and punctured lungs. The .44 Magnum killer had taken another life. Unknown to Sirgo and the rescue crew, Burl and Childress had already freed themselves from the elevator, sliding down its steel cables to the ground level.

The thermometer outside read in the mid-forties, while the French Market weathervane spun toward the north wind, making it feel even chillier. Retreating to a concrete cubicle on the southeast portion of the hotel roof, the sniper found cover and continued his onslaught, exchanging a barrage of gunfire with law enforcement. A voice cried out from the bullet-ridden cubbyhole, "Happy New Year's, pigs! I've killed four of you motherfuckers! Come on up, and I'll kill four more!"

A Jefferson Parish Sheriff's Office helicopter, a two-seater, was deployed into action with a deer rifle–toting deputy aboard. The chopper retreated when the sniper began shooting at it. From the Naval Air Station Joint Reserve Base in Belle Chasse, Marine Lieutenant Colonel Charles H. Pitman had had about enough of watching this disaster unfold on TV. One can imagine what was going on through his mind, "We arrived too late at the Rault Center. What are we waiting for?" A patriot who loved the sting of battle, Pitman took off without clearance on a Sea Knight Marine helicopter to assist the police officers. It was a cold, gray day. There was a steady rain that fell silently. By 3:30 p.m., fog had rolled in with a chance of snow. The sky darkened at around 5:30 p.m., as NOPD sharpshooters Frank Buras, Thomas Casey and Antoine Saacks and communications specialist Tony Buonagura boarded the Sea Knight from the Louisiana Superdome parking lot. (Dave Dixon's magnificent enclosed stadium, which soon became the largest in the world, was skeletal and in its infancy.)

Located at the Police Administration Complex at 715 South Broad Street in New Orleans, Sirgo Plaza serves as a memorial to NOPD Deputy Superintendent Louis J. Sirgo. It was dedicated on March 25, 1975. *Courtesy of The Historic New Orleans Collection.*

The men rode into battle in the big, tandem-rotor helicopter, enveloping the enemy's cubbyhole with a spotlight. On that first pass, no shots were fired from the cops. A strong odor of tear gas was detected around the cubicle, an earlier attempt to make the sniper break his cover. As the copter was pulling off, the sniper fired at it. A second and third pass involved the sharpshooters, armed with fully automatic AR-15s, and many other police on top of the Rault Center and Loyola and BNO buildings blasting away at the cubbyhole. Chunks of concrete flew everywhere. The structure looked like a war-scarred building from the Syrian Civil War. Somehow, the sniper managed to get out of their line of vision by shimmying up a water pipe inside the left rear corner of the cubicle. The sniper grew accustomed to the movements of the Sea Knight and would take shots at it when it was approaching or leaving. Around 9:00 p.m., a fourth pass was underway. The cubicle was once again littered with bullets, and they hoped some would ricochet and hit the blind spot that was protecting him. Sergeant Saacks reported seeing the water pipe explode from the ammo, cutting in half. As the helicopter began to leave, the sniper, shouting his final rebel yell while symbolically holding his right fist in the air, ran practically underneath the Sea Knight and drilled a shot near the transmission. As he was fully exposed, a hail of over two hundred bullets—with many saying it looked like a *Star Wars* laser battle—hit the sniper. The overkill was an admission of how inhuman this reign of terror was. Was he the lone gunman? Did he act alone? The plausible was deemed impossible.

Daybreak marked the 158th anniversary of the Battle of New Orleans. A blue tank decorated with four small flags blowing in the wind fueled up at the Shell station on O'Keefe and Poydras Streets. Its mission: to liberate the Downtown Howard Johnson's hotel. The CBD was a ghost town; five blocks were closed off. On the hotel's rooftop, over thirty cops formed a semicircle around the boiler room, convinced there's another gunman hiding inside. Amid the excitement, the officers forgot to bring the keys to open the doors. Unwilling to go back to fetch them, they blasted away at the metal edifice with their firearms. The ricochets injured nine policemen, and several believed it was another gunman shooting back! When the smoke cleared, it was apparent they were victims of friendly fire, and it was all broadcast live on the local news. In the stillness of a bitter cold morning, the gun battle was over.

Lieutenant Colonel Pitman served as the wings for the Ground Commander, NOPD Superintendent Giarrusso. With his mobile support, they had won this ugly war. Pitman made a total of forty-eight passes over the roof; his quick thinking and call to action had brought down the sniper the night before. Instead of being honored as a hero, he got chewed out by his superiors and faced the possibility of a court-martial, as he had used military resources and personnel to stop a municipal affair without first obtaining the proper authorization. U.S. Representative F. Edward Hebert of New Orleans, who headed the House Armed Services Committee, negotiated for Pitman and got him off the hook. In June 1973, Pitman was transferred out of the Crescent City. He was involved in another tragic international story in 1980, taking charge of the helicopter crews who attempted to rescue fifty-two Americans who were being held hostage in Iran. Eight military members died when one of the copters crashed in a sandstorm.

At a press conference on Tuesday, January 9, Giarrusso identified the lone sniper as twenty-three-year-old Mark Essex of Emporia, Kansas. The registration on the .44-caliber rifle, along with the FBI Identification Division's match of the gunman's prints to a military fingerprint card, led investigators to the recently court-martialed Navy veteran.

Essex had been court-martialed for going AWOL on October 19, 1970, and he was separated from his naval services on January 28, 1971. The naval air station's commanding officer labeled him as impulsive and said he flagrantly disregarded military authority.

Why did Essex go AWOL? According to his own testimony and that of Dr. Robert Hatcher, a lieutenant naval officer and dentist who had befriended the troubled dental technician, Essex was the victim of systemic racism in the Navy. He was bullied and harassed constantly. Standing at five foot, four inches tall, it is plausible to assume his short stature elevated this taunting.

Racial unrest was a reality in the Navy at that time. On October 11 and 12, 1972, there was a race riot aboard the aircraft carrier *Kitty Hawk* off the coast of Vietnam. Forty-six men were injured in the fighting. Twenty-one Black crewmen were flown home and court-martialed. A Congressional investigation, led by the chairman of the House Armed Services Subcommittee Floyd Hicks, decided the incident "consisted of unprovoked attacks" by Black men against White men.

Mark Essex's U.S. Navy photograph. *Courtesy of the New Orleans Police Department.*

Alma Montero, a civilian colleague at Dr. Hatcher's clinic, praised Essex's work ethic and sunny disposition. She noticed that a dark side of his personality emerged after his twenty-first birthday; he became sullen, a loner who lost his radiant smile. "He began to associate with some Black sailors, some of whom I think were rather bad companions for him," she said. One of those companions was New Orleanian Rodney Frank, a radical with ties to the Black Panther Party. Relocating to the Crescent City after his military setback, Essex reunited with his shipmate. When two unarmed Black Southern University students were shot and killed during a campus confrontation with law enforcement on November 16, 1972, Essex went into a mental tailspin, electing to go to war with the White race.

On January 3, 1973, a chilling handwritten letter from Essex was received by WWL-TV, New Orleans's CBS affiliate. In the note, he stated:

> *Africa greets you. On December 31, 1972* [approximately] *11 p.m., the Downtown New Orleans Police Department will be attacked. Reason—many. But the death of two innocent brothers will be avenged. And many others.*
>
> *P.S. Tell Pig Giarrusso the felony action squad ain't shit.*

The letter was signed "MATA," a Swahili word meaning "instrument to kill." The word *mata* was among other Black revolutionary sayings found scrawled across the walls of Essex's New Orleans apartment at 2619½ Dryades Street. Inside a bathroom closet, a map of New Orleans was discovered, with the police headquarters and the Downtown Howard Johnson's circled in black. The most immediate route from Essex's apartment to the hotel was marked. A 1973 horoscope book was also found inside the disturbing dwelling. There is a rumor that one of the representatives of NOPSI informed Giarrusso of where Essex resided.

Was the letter delayed in the mail? Based on its contents, it was presumably a warning of a New Year's Eve police station attack.

The letter was made public on January 29, 1973. What if it had been unveiled the day it was received, January 3? Could Essex's deadly rampage at the Downtown Howard Johnson's four days later have been halted by his capture?

Ballistics showed Essex had acted alone. In total, eighty-three .44 Magnum caliber shells were recovered from the hotel; fifty-one had been fired. Bullets taken from the bodies of Cadet Alfred Harrell, Dr. Steagall and Louis Sirgo were forensically matched to Essex's Ruger Carbine. He also used a .38-caliber Colt revolver in the attack. Thirty-four eyewitnesses testified to seeing Essex alone on or before January 7, 1973. He was never seen in the company of another person.

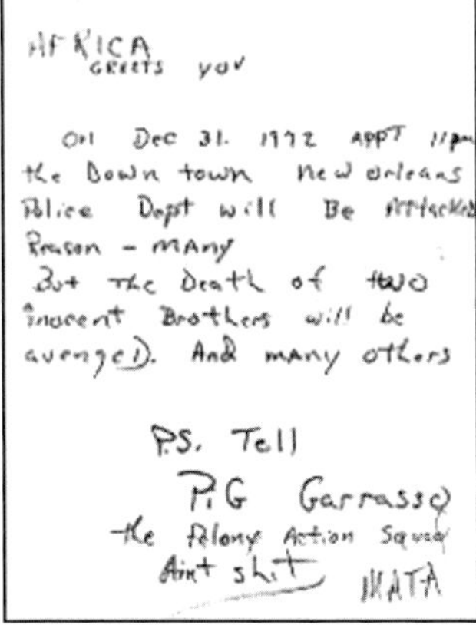
AFRICA greets you

On Dec 31. 1972 APPT 11pm the Down town New Orleans Police Dept will Be Attacked Reason - many But the Death of two innocent Brothers will be avenged). And many others

P.S. Tell Pig Garrasso the Felony Action Squad Ain't shit

MATA

Left: Mark Essex's letter to WWL. *Courtesy of the New Orleans Police Department.*

Right: The apartment walls of Mark Essex. *Courtesy of the New Orleans Police Department.*

According to Essex's mother, Nellie, her son showed no venomous attitude toward White people during his Kansas upbringing. In fact, he had dated a White girl. It was during his Navy days that she believed he changed.

In total, nine people were murdered by Essex; another ten were seriously wounded. Nine men had been shot by friendly fire, one person had suffered a heart attack and two others had sustained minor injuries.

Lawsuits totaling over $11 million were filed by relatives of the dead and guests of the hotel, who blamed the operator of the Downtown Howard Johnson's and other defendants of negligence. Two years later, a federal jury awarded damages of $275,000 to the victims; approximately half of it went to Mr. and Mrs. Robert V. Steagall Sr., the parents of the slain physician. An out-of-court settlement of $400,000 was awarded to Tim Ursin, the fireman who lost his hand.

In 1973, the NOPD did not have a SWAT (Special Weapons and Tactics) team. The Howard Johnson's sniper incident urged the demand for one. Around 1975, Nick Congemi led a group of Kenner officers to the FBI training center in Quantico for SWAT training. They were the second in the state to be certified in such tactics by the FBI. The NOPD founded its SWAT team in April 1979, under the direction of Captain Calvin Galliano.

The UpStairs Lounge Fire (June 24, 1973)

The storage and office space of the Jimani, a French Quarter bar established in 1971, seems to be a typical storehouse at first glance. Char marks on the wall remind us of a horrific evening that occurred here over a quarter of a century ago. The place is a labyrinth of rooms and stairwells. It is hard to believe that the worst mass murder of gay people in U.S. history, prior to the Orlando Pulse Nightclub shooting of 2016, happened here.

The French Quarter is one of the most popular vacation spots in America. People from around the world visit this European treasure nestled in the Deep South. Hidden in the corners, among the romance and mystique, are tragic stories that define the area. The Good Friday Fire of 1788 that destroyed more than eight hundred houses and public buildings within hours began on the corner of Chartres and Toulouse Streets at the home of Don Vincente Jose Nuñez. The Catholic Church took a lot of blame for the tragedy; priests were slow to ring the church bells to warn the citizens. Catholic doctrine does not permit church bells to ring on Good Friday.

Around 185 years later, on the same street, at the corner of Chartres and Iberville Streets, the deadliest twentieth-century New Orleans fire occurred at the UpStairs Lounge. Once again, a Nuñez was connected to the blaze.

Summers in New Orleans are extremely hot and humid, and the summer of 1973 was no exception. Snowballs, also known as snow cones around the United States, were eagerly consumed at Wilson's snowball stand near the I-610 exit on Elysian Fields in Gentilly. Three middle-aged, sweaty men brandishing icepicks and knives unloaded blocks of ice from a green pickup truck at the establishment; they had gotten the ice from the icehouse on Gentilly Boulevard, near the Baptist seminary. Snowballs were invented in the Crescent City; they are a favorite local treat during the season.

City Park entertained baseball games and animal shows. The Superdome was being constructed at the time, ushering in progress in a recession-torn country. Gas was scarce, and local businesses were suffering. Meat prices were skyrocketing, affecting restaurants. By and large, Black and White residents in lower Algiers appeared to be unhappy with the school board's decision to allow busing in neighborhoods.

Amid these uncertain, turbulent times, the Harlem Globetrotters were putting smiles on people's faces, performing their magic at the RKO Orpheum Theater show on June 24. Attorney Harold Bartholomew, who was thirty-three years old at the time, and his three young children attended the Globetrotters' event. Their short ride home from the French Quarter to Metairie was their longest journey together. The well-dressed and charismatic lawyer reflected on his time at the foreboding location:

> *I was trying to get across the street, and the taxi in front of me stopped, and the explosion had happened—*boom! *And it hit us at the side of the car; I made the kids put the windows up and get on the floor. I think I bumped the taxi to move him along; he was just mesmerized. I got across the street, and then we drove on. By that time, the place was in full flames. There were bars on the windows, and people were at the windows, cooking. It's the only way to describe it. And they were reaching out, and they couldn't get out, because the windows were barred.*
>
> *The strongest image I ever had was the two guys walking out of the lounge door—the brownish, blond-haired guy (the shorter one) and the guy in back of him, crouched down. What he said was, "That'll teach the motherfuckers!" And they walked on. I tried to follow them, but I was too interested in getting across.*
>
> *Some of the people trapped were without pieces, squeezing through the bars, hitting the ground, burning. They couldn't come down the steps; the steps was an inferno. It was like looking into a doorway to hell. It was nothing but flames. Undoubtedly, that was gasoline.*

The fire was intentionally set on the stairway of the UpStairs Lounge entrance. At 7:52 p.m., the bell on the lounge's front door started ringing nonstop. Irritated with the noise, a patron opened the lounge's entrance door at the top of the stairs. A strong backdraft exploded into the bar area. The blaze then spread into the lounge. Smoke damage was found inside the theater; the fire door was closed to stop the spread of the fire. Twenty-eight bodies were discovered at the UpStairs Lounge after the fire. Of those who escaped, one died before reaching the hospital, three died later of burn injuries and seven others were critically burned. Bartender Buddy Rasmussen led about twenty people to safety through the theater's fire

Glancing at the second story of the Jimani, the former location of the UpStairs Lounge, Harold Bartholomew revisits his nightmare. *Author's collection.*

Two bodies by the UpStairs Lounge window. *Courtesy of Johnny Townsend.*

door exit, located behind the stage. Only about one-third of the occupants followed the barkeeper through the theater. The remainder were in a panic to reach the windows.

Phil Esteve opened the UpStairs Lounge on Halloween in 1970; it was a gay bar brimming with an eclectic range of patrons: intellectuals, actors, poets, musicians, doctors and vagabonds. The jukebox, filled with 45s customers had donated, had music ranging from rock-and-roll to opera.

The lounge functioned as a meeting place for the Metropolitan Community Church, a universal denomination committed to serving the gay, lesbian and transgender community. Many members were at the lounge the evening of the fire, planning a benefit for the Crippled Children's Hospital.

As authorities investigated, Reverend Bill Larson's body was visible from the street for hours after the fire, appearing on *The States-Item*'s front page the following day. Assistant pastor Mitch Mitchell eluded the fire but ran back into the building to save his partner, Horace Broussard. Both perished in the fire.

Mitch was from northeast Alabama, a land rich in scenery and natural beauty. The historic Trail of Tears corridor coincidentally runs through the town of Rainsville, the home of Mitch's son, Duane. He reflected on the memories of his dad, now pressed between the pages of his mind:

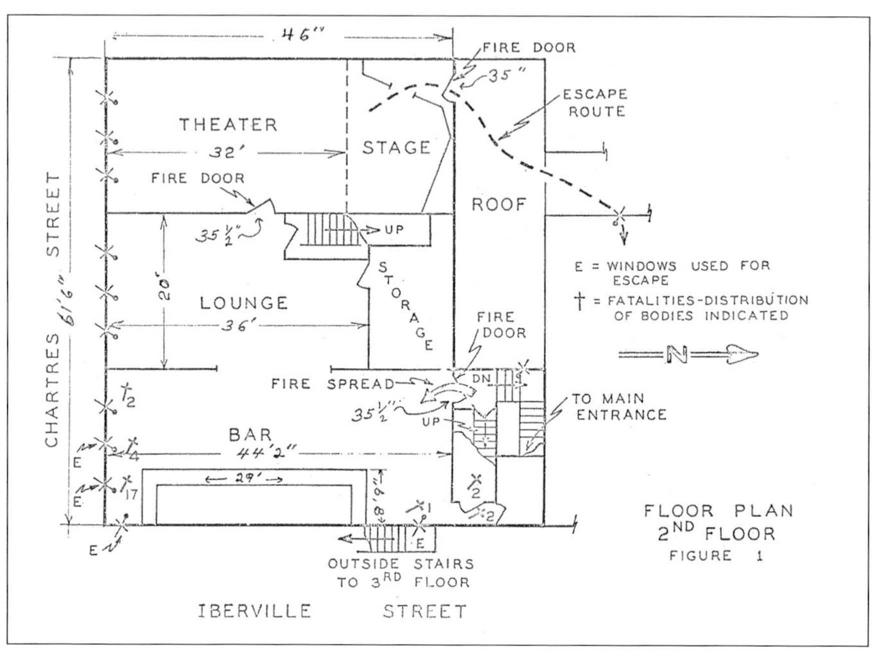

Diagram of the UpStairs Lounge Fire. *Courtesy of the NFPA.*

Left: Buddy Rasmussen. *Courtesy of Johnny Townsend.*

Right: Phil Esteve. *Courtesy of Johnny Townsend.*

Buddy Rasmussen in costume at Mardi Gras, 1973. The interior design at the UpStairs: beefcake photographs of Burt Reynolds and Mark Spitz and flocked wallpaper. *Courtesy of Johnny Townsend.*

A Nelly drama performed at the UpStairs. *Courtesy of Johnny Townsend.*

Above: Mitch Mitchell (*left*) and Horace Broussard (*right*). *Courtesy of Johnny Townsend.*

Right: In life: Reverend Bill Larson, a World War II veteran. *Courtesy of Johnny Townsend.*

Opposite, top: In death: Reverend Bill Larson. Author Robert Fieseler spearheaded the effort to get a marker on Larson's unmarked crypt at St. Roch Cemetery in New Orleans. The author of this book joined the endeavor and petitioned the Department of Veteran Affairs. An official military plaque was placed on his tomb shortly afterward in 2018. *Courtesy of* The Times-Picayune.

Mitch Mitchell as Queen Victoria at Mardi Gras, 1973. *Courtesy of Johnny Townsend.*

When I was five years old, he put me on a piano bench at church, and I sung my first song. He loved going to the gospel singings, the dinners on the ground, homecomings, when he was here. He had some old cars the bulls didn't like very much. He'd park in the pastures; he had one car, and a bull attacked it. It was neat! It was an ugly car; it wasn't red though!

Mitch and his wife, Vicki, were divorced. He moved to Panama City Beach, Florida, and then to New Orleans. In 1973, Duane, who was eleven, and Steve, who was eight, visited their dad that summer. The waning crescent glowed, unveiling the horror of that unfathomable evening. Duane addressed that night he lost his dad:

Well, he was wanting to go….He never didn't say where—he just said he was going to this place, and he was gonna drop us off at the theater and come back and get us. And that wasn't the first time he ever done it. The movie was The World's Greatest Athlete, *and we watched it a total of seven times that night. There wasn't nobody there much but me and my brother and the people who owned the theater. And we was waiting on Dad to come, but he never did. The landlady come and got us and took us to an apartment, and then the guy next door the next day took us to Pontchartrain Beach. Then, we flew back home; they put us on a jet and flew us to Atlanta Airport. Granddaddy and them picked us up and brought us back.*

Mitch's remains were identified a week later. Funeral arrangements had to be made. Duane added:

My granddaddy left it up to me. He asked me if I wanted to pick out the stuff or wanted him to do it, and I said, "No, I can do it." And I did. I remember it was a blue coffin with white interior. I picked out the casket, the place where he was supposed to be buried and the preacher who did the service. I was eleven years old. I'll never forget that. And they put a picture of him on top of the casket, because they couldn't open it; he was burned so bad.

Well, I think he was a hero. And it would only be my dad that would do that, because he was always that kind of person. He cared about people and their feelings. I got mad at him one time. He was visiting, and he'd been getting on to me a lot. I said, "What did I do now?" He just looked at me and started crying and said, "I'm sorry son; I didn't mean to get on you so much." He was just that kind of person. He was gentle…a kind and gentle person, and he's a hero. No matter what anybody says, I think he's a hero.

Terry Gilbert was a rookie firefighter of only two weeks, working three tours before he was called to the UpStairs Lounge. From his sprawling Slidell home, Gilbert's two showroom classic Corvettes became an instant distant memory, and he told his account of the fire:

> *Traffic, for some unknown reason, was very heavy. We turned on Royal Street; there were people trying to get out of our way. We actually hit two taxicabs and drove them up on the sidewalks because our deputy chief was on the corner, waving us up, telling us all, "Don't worry about the accident! Come on down! I need the water pronto!" The fire was only three blocks from our engine house; we had to circumvent the French Quarter to get to it, whereas we couldn't buck traffic.*
>
> *The fire was coming from the second story, hence the name the UpStairs Lounge. There was a lot of confusion, people screaming. We tried to go about our task and get water on the fire. As I recall, the fire was put under control very quickly, like in sixteen minutes. Under control is not out, but under control meaning it can't spread any further.*
>
> *There were bars on all of the windows, and when we got inside, we noticed that their fire door was chained closed. Their fire started from an interior stairwell. There was one way up, and there was a rear entrance which was chained closed. Their firebomb was set in the interior stairwell, and inside, there were a lot of elaborate decorations and stuff that burned readily. They were pretty much trapped.*

According to the National Fire Protection Association's report, Rasmussen had locked the fire door to prevent the spread of the fire after leading approximately twenty people to safety. This act unintentionally left the remaining bar patrons with no escape route. Gilbert continued:

> *The thing that I remember most was there were sections of the building's interior, and there were piles of people close to the bathroom, close to a window, close to the fire escape door. When you were a child, you ever played tackle the man with the ball, where everyone piles on the ball carrier? That's kind of what it looked like—in a grotesque way.*
>
> *We called in the coroner, who came in with prisoners from Orleans Parish Prison, and some of the firefighters actually helped load the bodies into the bags. It was horrible. No one deserved to die that way. No one.*

Identifying the bodies proved to be a difficult task, as evidenced by this 1973 WVUE interview with NOPD Sergeant Joseph Vitari:

> *We have got dental charts sent in from all over the country on twelve people so far. The FBI, where they come in real good, is that we can send the names to Washington, they find out who these people are and what city they from. They contact the officials in this city and find out where these people lived and find out what dentist they went to. And they contacted the dentists; they have the dentists send us the dental charts. And that and fingerprints would be the only true way we can identify these people. It's impossible for a mother to look at her son and say that's her son; that's how badly burned the bodies are.*

Three victims were buried in unmarked graves at Resthaven Cemetery on Gentilly Road, unclaimed, unidentified and unwanted.

For a prolonged period after the fire, scholars and the general public believed the unknown fire victims were buried at the Holt Cemetery beside Delgado Community College. In 2014, through a lot of microfilm research at the University of New Orleans, this author discovered their burial spot was not at Holt but at Resthaven.

Californian Marilyn LeBlanc Downey found out her long-lost brother Ferris LeBlanc, a World War II veteran, was one of the victims interred there. His exact burial spot in the open field, Q-32, is included in a cemetery diagram. This map, along with video footage of the burial included in this author's 2013 documentary *The UpStairs Lounge Fire* (the first film ever produced about this tragedy), are the only clues for finding Ferris. He hasn't been found yet.

Gareth Griffin's 2008 History thesis at the University of Louisiana at Lafayette, "Flames of Hate: The New Orleans UpStairs Lounge Fire, 24 June 1973," exposed the rampant homophobia present during the time of the fire. Homosexuality was included in the American Psychiatric Association's *Diagnostic and Statistical Manual of Mental Disorders*. It was removed in December 1973, six months after the UpStairs Lounge fire. The 1974 Louisiana Crime Against Nature statute made sexual acts between homosexual couples illegal. Underneath this umbrella of antipathy, Louisiana Governor Edwin Edwards and New Orleans Mayor Moon Landrieu made no public announcement expressing sympathy for the victims of the fire.

St. Mark's United Methodist Church was the only church in New Orleans to hold a memorial service for the victims of the fire. Additionally,

Left: Dr. Perry Waters, a dentist who perished in the fire. Records from his office were used to identify the bodies. *Courtesy of Johnny Townsend.*

Right: Rodger Nunez's Abbeville High School yearbook photograph. When he was twenty-six years old, Nunez was the prime suspect in the UpStairs Lounge fire. *Courtesy of Johnny Townsend.*

Father Bill Richardson held a small prayer service for the victims at St. George's Episcopal Church, but he was later chastised by his superiors for doing so. Contrary to popular belief spread by rumors, Archbishop Philip Hannan did offer prayers and consolation for the victims in a piece he wrote that was included in the July 19, 1973 issue of the *Clarion Herald*, the official newspaper of the Archdiocese of New Orleans. Adam Fontenot, Buddy Rasmussen's partner, received a Catholic funeral at Sacred Heart of Jesus Catholic Church in Ville Platte, Louisiana. Three Catholic priests were photographed praying for and blessing fire victims outside of the lounge by *States-Item* photographer G.E. Arnold. The photograph was printed on page A-6a in the June 25, 1973 issue. AP Pulitzer Prize–winning photographer Jack Thornell was also at the scene and took a similar photograph of three priests.

Lab tests confirmed the blaze was caused by arson. An empty can of lighter fluid was discovered at the base of the lounge's entrance stairwell.

The steps were wooden and carpeted, a direct violation of the National Fire Protection Code. Although this arson remains unsolved, one suspect, Rodger Nunez, stands out.

Johnny Townsend's book about the UpStairs Lounge fire, *Let the Faggots Burn: The UpStairs Lounge Fire*, is widely considered the most comprehensive compilation of firsthand accounts of the fire. Speaking from his porch, high on a hill in Columbia City, Seattle, the pioneer of UpStairs Lounge fire research reflected on his analysis of the tragedy:

> *It's not officially concluded who set the fire, but all evidence points to Rodger Nunez. He was a gay guy who was in the bar causing trouble, got kicked out of the bar, got punched by a guy and fractured his jaw. Michael Scarborough told me Rodger Nunez looked up at him from the floor and said, "I'm gonna burn you guys out!" And then the fire started just a few minutes later, so it seems pretty clear that's what happened.*
>
> *I talked to Miss Fury; she's a really tall, strikingly red-haired transgender woman who told me Rodger confessed to her. Now, I just have her word for it, but I also read the transcripts of the investigation, and Rodger failed his lie detector test, and his friends failed lie detector tests. How accurate those lie detector tests were, I don't know, but again, it's just another piece of circumstantial evidence that points to him.*
>
> *There's a plaque right outside the UpStairs Lounge in the French Quarter now that says how this was a turning point in gay rights in New Orleans, and I really don't think that's the case. No one I interviewed who talked about the things that went on at that time suggested that at all. I think the turning point for gay rights in New Orleans was Anita Bryant, later in the mid-1970s, when she was doing all of her anti-gay rhetoric. But I don't think the UpStairs Lounge changed anything. One person, Stewart Butler, who was a regular at the bar, told me, "It was a terrible tragedy that no good came out of."*

Soon after the fire, Nunez married Elaine Wharton and moved to New Orleans East. He committed suicide at their home on November 15, 1974, a little over a year after the UpStairs Lounge fire. Nunez was buried at Harrington Cemetery, near Forked Island. This genteel resting place strongly contrasts with Nunez's vagrant lifestyle in New Orleans prior to his marriage.

Dr. Clayton Delery's award-winning book *The UpStairs Lounge Arson: Thirty-Two Deaths in a New Orleans Gay Bar, June 24, 1973* examines why justice was denied. Sipping on a cool glass of ice water with a lemon wedge al fresco at Sake Cafe in Elmwood, Delery delivered three important insights:

I'm not a lawyer, I'm not a prosecutor for sure, but it seems to me if one of three things had happened during Rodger's life, the case might have been solved. And that is if there were fingerprints on the can of lighter fluid that was found in the stairwell and they matched Rodger's, the case could have been solved. If the woman who sold the lighter fluid to a man who matches his general description had been able to pick his photograph out of a photo lineup, it might have been solved, or if one of his friends had come forward during his life and said, "When Rodger is drunk, he sometimes says he started the fire, and then when he sobers up, he denies it," that could have closed the case. I think any one of those three things could've done it, but none of those things happened. And because none of those things happened, that leaves open the possibility that he didn't do it.

A group photograph at the UpStairs. *Courtesy of Johnny Townsend.*

A Mardi Gras costume contest at the UpStairs, 1973. *Courtesy of Johnny Townsend.*

The back room of the UpStairs served as a theater. Mike Scarborough (*left*), Ginny Lynch (*center*) and Reggie Adams (*right*) await curtain time. Scarborough was a survivor of the fire. Adams was one of the thirty-two victims who died. *Courtesy of Johnny Townsend.*

Consolidated lawsuits arose against the City of New Orleans. In 1975, Civil District Judge Gerald Fedoroff ruled in favor of the city; only the arsonist was at fault. His ruling was upheld in 1977 at the Fourth Circuit Court of Appeal. An out-of-court settlement of $80,000 was allocated among the plaintiffs, a combination of liability insurance and the cash obtained from the building's owner, Anthony Gaurino.

Artist Skylar Fine's 2008 installation, *Remember the UpStairs Lounge*, was shown as part of the biennial Prospect 1 New Orleans. Fine reconstructed the history of the fire through his artwork and photographs. The New Orleans Museum of Art acquired the postmodern installation in 2013. Fine's sentiments were illuminating:

> *And in fact, the people who died were living! They were having a gay ole' time; they were drinking beer, listening to music, and they were singing and dancing, and I thought we should honor that, too. That's okay to remember that they were living and living it up, as a matter of fact, in their own way. And I thought, well, we're still alive. Let's not pretend we're dead; we ain't dead yet! And that's why I have music playing in the installation, and I have some kitschy artifacts from 1973. It's okay to smile and laugh when we think about their lives.*

3

TWO MAJOR TRAGEDIES ON THE MISSISSIPPI IN A LITTLE OVER A YEAR

The Luling Ferry Disaster (October 20, 1976): The Worst Ferryboat Accident in U.S. History

The Mississippi River at dawn—cool air, murky waters—is a juxtaposition between natural beauty and industrial prowess. The Mississippi River's résumé includes such notable people as Mark Twain, whose name bespeaks of his pilot days. The beauty of the river has inspired the creation of many small towns along the riverbanks in Louisiana: Luling, Destrehan, Kenner, LaPlace and Norco, just to name a few. Majestic plantations on River Road remind visitors of how the past is still alive.

In the 1970s, Louisiana was enjoying economic success that had never been imagined in the area before. Governor Edwin Edwards used oil boom dollars to boost social spending, and he rewrote the state constitution. He was best known for his charm and flair—not his humility. If you asked him who the greatest Louisiana politician ever was, his answer would be: "In my lifetime, it would have to be every time I shave and look in the mirror, I see him."

The week of October 16, 1976, seemed to start off normally. At Joy's Cinema City 6 in Kenner, Woody Allen's *Love and Death* was featured, as well as two maritime films: *The Sailor Who Fell from Grace with the Sea* and *Treasure Island*. It's almost like the filmmakers had an eerie premonition.

Born in New York City in 1941, Egidio "Gene" Auletta was a U.S. Air Force veteran with an array of occupations in his lifetime. In 1961, he was a dance instructor in Tacoma, Washington. Auletta was issued a U.S. FAA private pilot's license, airplane single engine land, in 1968, when he was living in Mobile, Alabama. *Courtesy of Kelly Auletta Harris.*

It was 40° Fahrenheit and dark at dawn on Wednesday, October 20, 1976, as the fifty-year-old *George Prince* ferry was making its way across the Mississippi River from Destrehan to Luling. The skipper was Captain Gene Auletta, who was thirty-five years old and relatively new to the ferry operation on the river. What's more, he was working the midnight shift. The ferry was packed tight with automobiles. Pedestrians walked onto the crowded boat, filling the passenger room. Ninety-four people were aboard that morning, most of them young men who worked on the plants along the riverbank.

At 6:12 a.m., as the *George Prince* traveled close to a mile from the east bank to the west bank, a twenty-two-thousand-ton Norwegian tanker, the *Frosta*, sighted the ferry dangerously close to the front of the ship's bow. Pilot Nicholas Colombo of the *Frosta* signaled to the *George Prince* with two whistle blasts—no reply. At 6:13 a.m., the *Frosta* signaled again, "DANGER"—no reply. At 6:15 a.m. and still signaling, Colombo's notes read "FULL ASTERN."

Passengers aboard the *George Prince* frantically sounded their horns and flashed their headlights, trying to alert their captain to the gigantic crisis approaching. It seemed as if almost everyone aboard knew of the danger, except for the pilot, Auletta. Some grabbed life jackets and clung onto the rail for dear life; they were trying to brace themselves for a massive collision, but most of the souls aboard were already doomed. The *George Prince* cut right in front of the *Frosta*.

Charles Chatelain, who worked at the Texaco plant at the time, was on the doomed vessel that fateful morning. With the assistance of cinematographer Melissa Hauck, this author interviewed him for his master's thesis documentary project at the University of Louisiana at Lafayette on Saturday, August 27, 2005, at the site of the former Destrehan ferry landing. Two days later, Hurricane Katrina decimated Greater New Orleans. The following is Chatelain's account:

Collision illustration. *Illustration by Nathan Henry.*

While I was sitting in my truck, I heard a man say, "It's gonna hit!" And I didn't know what he meant; I just kind of thought it would be barges out in the river.

The ship hit the ferry, and as I'm sitting behind the wheel of the truck, the collision bounced me off the passenger door, and I came back up over the steering wheel, and I was in my windshield. Once I was in my windshield, then I saw the ship coming, and before I could reach over and get the door, I was in the water. Right before I went in the water, with the ship coming straight for me, I saw the ship running all over the people that were in the passenger room. And I just saw that ship coming straight for me, and of course, when you're down in the river and you're looking at the seven-hundred-foot-long ship, it looks like One Shell Square coming down on you.

As the truck went down, I couldn't see anything, but I could hear the roar of the ship above, and I could also feel other vehicles starting to bump into my truck.

Entombed in their automobiles, heading toward their watery grave, Chatelain also heard the death wails of other ferry travelers. With Chatelain descending deeper and deeper into the river, his entire life and family flashed right in front of him. Suddenly, at a depth of about sixty-five feet, his windshield gave way and busted. He asserted: "Once it blew out, it shot me like a cannon out of the truck, and it shot me a good ten or twelve feet into the river, and I was going straight up."

With cars and drums falling on top of him as he ascended, something even stranger happened. Chatelain explained:

> *As I was coming up, I felt a hand come in my hand, but I couldn't feel a body attached to it, and eventually I just let it go, because I still didn't feel a body attached to it. By then, I was starting to suck in some water because I couldn't hold my breath anymore, and I could feel diesel fuel and water going down my throat. I didn't take big gulps; I took very, very small sips, and then, all of sudden, I came up, and my head was above water. The first thing I saw was the rear end of the* Frosta, *and I knew that if you get too close to the back end of the ship, it sucks you in, so I swam out in the middle of the river and away from the ship, and I swam as far as I could.*

Chatelain was in good shape. He swam three miles at the gym every week. Even with the weight of his work boots, coat and overalls and the strong undercurrent of the Mississippi, his strength and tenacity overcame death's odds. In Chatelain's words:

> *I tried to relax on my back and couldn't do it because the river just took me right back under. So, when I came up, what I thought was a barge was actually the ferry. The ferry was 110 feet long, and it went straight down into the river, which was 100 feet. So, they had eight or ten feet of ferry sticking up out of the river, and I swam a good ways to get to it. Once I got to the ferry, I can promise you I've never thrown up in my life, but I threw up all over the place, several times, because I could feel that diesel and river water in me, and my throat was burning, and I was freezing from the water, and I climbed aboard the ferry. As soon as I did, they had another ferryboat out there, and it flashed its lights on me and told me through a loudspeaker that they were coming to get me and take me to the hospital. When they recovered my truck, they pulled everything out of there; it was like an accordion, and they said everything was on top of it,*

Top: Charles Chatelain. *Author's collection.*

Bottom: The capsized ferry. *Courtesy of the* St. Charles Herald-Guide.

> *so if I'd of stayed in it, I'd of just been crushed. And like I say, if you call it divine intervention or whatever, but something happened to make me lucky enough to get out.*

Meanwhile, a few miles away from the crossing between Destrehan and Luling, two parents were about to be taken by surprise. Kenneth and Iris Songy wondered if their twenty-three-year old son, Richard, who rode the ferry every day to work, was aboard the crushed ship. Kenneth reflected on that dreadful day: "That morning, I was going to work; I was going in for six o'clock, and I heard that the ferry had been hit, but it never dawned on me that my son would've been on the ferry at that time, cause normally, he went to work earlier in the morning."

Around 6:45 a.m., Kenneth got a call from his wife, Iris, telling him that Richard may have been aboard the boat. The couple then rushed over to the town of Norco to be with Richard's newlywed wife and baby, awaiting news on whether he was on the ferry or not. Iris spoke: "In the afternoon, they said they had brought up the first person, and it was our son that was brought up first. I had kept praying for him to let him come up soon, and the Lord was very good, and he did. He was the first one to come up."

Left: Richard Songy. *Courtesy of Kenneth and Iris Songy.*

Right: Kenneth and Iris Songy at their home in St. Rose. Iris was the first teacher to open a kindergarten in St. Charles Parish, three years before kindergarten was available in the public school system. Kenneth was a World War II veteran, earning the Asiatic-Pacific Campaign Ribbon, the Good Conduct Medal, the Army of Occupation Ribbon–Japan, the Victory Ribbon and two Overseas Service Bars. *Author's collection.*

The mystery diver who brought up Richard was revealed to Iris only weeks before this interview with her, at a video store by a clerk who knew about the accident. "Well, how did you lose your son?" she asked. Iris replied, "He drowned in the ferry accident; he was the first one to be brought up and the first one to be buried." The clerk remarked, "Oh! Do you know my husband is the one that brought him up?"

Judging from the bump on Richard's head, he had been knocked unconscious from the impact of the accident. Others who were locked inside their cars weren't so fortunate; scratch marks were discovered inside many of the vehicles, where desperate escape attempts had failed.

Kenneth and Iris's strong Catholic faith strengthened even more the day after the accident, but it was not only Catholics who comforted them.

The Songys naturally turned to their faith and found words of reassurance in the Old Testament. In her spare time, Iris creates rosaries from Job's tears that Kenneth grows in his garden. Her closing thoughts were encouraging:

> *I went to the Bible and found Isaiah 43: "When you pass through the water, I will be with you. In the rivers, you shall not drown."*
>
> *And that meant so much to me. Even though he drowned, I knew he wasn't gone just nowhere. The Lord had taken him on up to heaven to be with him.*

Archbishop Hannan of New Orleans established a temporary morgue for the victims at the Knights of Columbus Hall in Norco. He also celebrated a

The turned-over ferry with a rescuer on its top. *Courtesy of* The Times-Picayune.

Mass of Resurrection for the ferry victims at Norco's Sacred Heart Catholic Church. Greater New Orleans has a high concentration of Catholics. His words to the grieving loved ones eased their concerns:

> *And the spiritual message for the survivors is that these people had enough time to make an Act of Contrition before they died, and that took care of their spiritual future. They certainly, regardless of how excited they were, regardless of whether or not they could form any words, they had the right attitude, they had the right intention of being sorry for their sins and meeting their creator.*

With the death count at seventy-seven and only eighteen survivors, a Coast Guard board of investigations sought to find out who had the right-of-way, the *Frosta* or the *George Prince* ferry. The ferry captain, Auletta, died in the accident, but the *Frosta*'s captain, Colombo, lived to testify and told how the ferry kept coming over and that there was absolutely nothing the tanker could do. He also said it was general practice and common sense for ferries and smaller vessels to give way to larger ships, especially since they have more room to maneuver.

But it was Orleans Parish Coroner Dr. Frank Minyard's autopsy report on skipper Auletta that made the picture even clearer; the ferry captain had been drinking, and tests showed he was just one-one-hundredth of a percent below the legal limit for drunkenness.

In 1972, just out of law school, Daniel Becnel Jr. won the first million-dollar personal injury jury trial in Louisiana. *Author's collection.*

Lawsuits naturally ensued. Daniel Becnel Jr., who leads one of the most widely recognized class-action and mass tort firms in the country, filed actions on behalf of many of the victims' families.

From his River Road office in Reserve, the plain-spoken lawyer who was dressed for the tropics was enveloped by 1970s wood paneling adorned with pink and yellow Post-it notes. His desk, flooded with litigation papers, exemplified Becnel's need for a loyal, senior citizen secretary—no need for a computer at his post. Framed photographs of Becnel with Presidents Bill Clinton and Ronald Reagan caught this author's eye as the king of torts spoke about the case and its ramifications: "The state owned the riverboat. A private enterprise owned the big tanker vessel. So, the plaintiffs and their families sued both, and both contributed ultimately to the settlement."

Attorney Gordon Grant, who specializes in maritime law, defended the state in the case. Grant expounded on the legal quagmires of the probe:

> *At that time, the western rivers rules provided, at that time, that the ferry, crossing from the right side of the ship to the left side of the ship, was the privileged vessel; it had the right-of-way under the rules as they existed at that time, and the ferry, as the privileged vessel, was legally obligated to maintain its course and speed. The ship was the burdened vessel, and the ship was legally obligated to reduce speed and take other appropriate action as necessary to avoid collision.*

Judge Alvin Rubin, who, in addition to being a judge, taught law at Louisiana State University (LSU), presided over the case. Becnel expressed his admiration of Rubin:

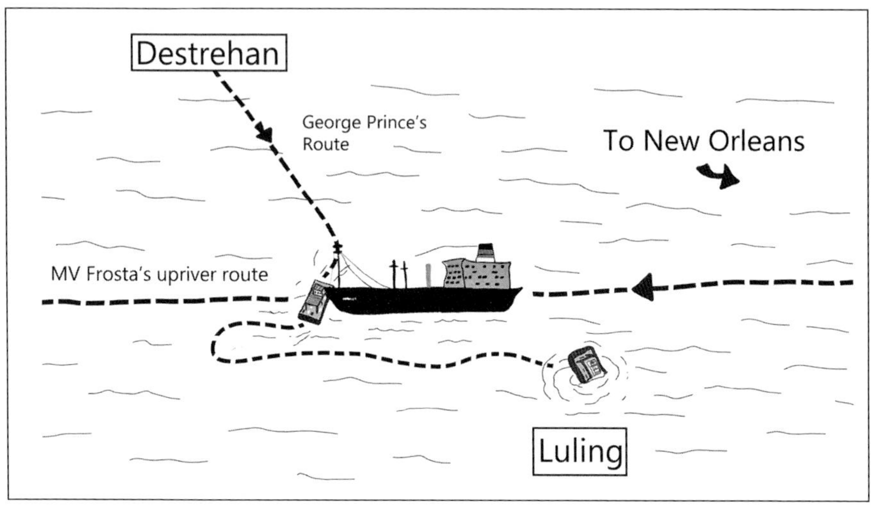

Diagram of the accident. *Illustration by Nathan Henry.*

> *Rubin, to me, did such a service to the families, because at the end of that year, all of the families had been paid; they didn't have to worry for six years or eight years, "How am I my going to feed my family? How am I going to send my kids to college?" when you had all of these widows and things like that. That's one of the things that I think Judge Fallon and most of the lawyers that were involved in that case—we call it the Rubin Rule: to try to get the case over quick.*

After the legal settlements, Judge Rubin made a special request to the family members' lawyers. Becnel continued: "Judge Rubin said, 'You plaintiff lawyers, I don't want you, now that you've got this case settled, to forget these victims, and I'd like you to do something, out of your pockets, to remember these victims.'"

A monument was erected at the St. John the Baptist Parish Courthouse in the small town of Edgard. Becnel and six other plaintiffs' attorneys put up 30 percent of the cost of the $30,000 monument; the State of Louisiana paid for 70 percent. There were several religious denominations among the victims, so an obelisk shape was chosen. The town of Edgard is about fifteen miles away from the crash site, which infuriated many of the victims' families. Most of the victims were from the East Bank in St. Charles Parish, so many wondered why the monument was on the West Bank in St. John Parish.

Judge Alvin Rubin. *Courtesy of Mike Beeman.*

Dolores Pritchett, who lost her sixteen-year-old son, Kevin, in the accident, was left confused, along with her son Tommy, by the monument's location. Sadly, Dolores and Tommy were arrested by the St. Charles police for public intimidation on the day of the accident. Why? To the parish police's chagrin, Tommy and other residents had gotten onto a private boat to conduct their own search and rescue effort. A verbal altercation between Dolores and the officers on the ferry landing led to their incarceration. The charges were later dropped.

Sitting beside his mother on their wine-colored couch, decorated with a Destrehan High School throw blanket, Tommy expressed his sentiments: "We would like to try to bring or get a monument here." Dolores interjected, "Yeah, because it belongs on the East Bank, and it belongs in St. Charles Parish." Tommy pressed on, "And one of the things we'd like to try to look at is maybe try and get a monument at the East Bank Bridge Park, which is only about a half-mile from where the ferry used to land."

Becnel attempted to place the monument at the St. Charles Parish Courthouse, but they refused, claiming it would be too painful a reminder. Several St. Charles officials said the monument site was changed because the old St. Charles Police Jury didn't want to give Becnel an advantage in his race against District Attorney Harry Morel in 1978.

On March 24, 1979, the National Transportation Safety Board said the major cause of the accident was the deficient maneuvering judgment of the ferry master, Captain Gene Auletta.

The Luling Ferry Disaster has had some lasting effects. In 1976, the Coast Guard did not subject pilots and other employees on vessels to random drug and alcohol testing; today, they are. Also, drug and alcohol testing is now required immediately after a collision. There has been a significant statistical reduction of these kinds of accidents as a result of these regulations. Ships in the river now legally have the right-of-way.

In 1983, the Hale Boggs Memorial Bridge was completed, ending the Destrehan–Luling ferry run. What was once the Destrehan landing is now private property.

From top to bottom:

The *George Prince* Ferry Memorial. *Author's collection.*

Archbishop Philip Hannan with the author's mother, Aida Anderson, and Kenneth Songy at the *George Prince* Ferry Memorial Ceremony on October 17, 2009. *Courtesy of Sid Anderson.*

The author at the *George Prince* Ferry Memorial Ceremony with his family and friends. *Left side of the table, front to back*: Marie Argence, Aida Anderson, the author, Isabelle Anderson and Grace Leleux (associate producer of the documentary). *Right side of the table, front to back*: Luke, Mark and Summer Anderson. Summer created the cover of this book, as well as the DVD covers for all the author's documentaries. *Courtesy of Sid Anderson.*

Since 2011, the *George Prince* ferry bell has been on permanent display at the East Bank Regional Library in Destrehan. Many thanks to Greg Lambousy for getting the bell there. It was in storage at the Cabildo, where Lambousy served as the director of collections. *Front, from left to right*: Luke and Ben Anderson. *Back, from left to right*: the author and Isabelle Anderson. *Courtesy of Sid Anderson.*

Recovery efforts of the sunken *George Prince*. *Courtesy of* L'Observateur.

Conferring about the expected number of casualties rescuers would eventually discover from the collision. *From left to right*: John O. St. Amant, St. Charles Parish Sheriff; Lieutenant Raymond Nuccio of the St. John the Baptist Parish Sheriff's Office; and Sheriff Lloyd B. Johnson of St. John. *Courtesy of* L'Observateur.

A rare photograph of the *George Prince* after the collision, floating on the river—notice its destroyed railing. *Courtesy of* L'Observateur.

Recovery efforts of the sunken *George Prince*. *Courtesy of* L'Observateur.

Fred Hurt at Sunday dinner at the Andersons on March 27, 2011. Before his fame on the Discovery Channel, Hurt was a diver who helped in the ferry disaster recovery efforts. *From left to right*: the author, Aida Anderson, Fred Hurt and Eric Anderson. *Courtesy of Sid Anderson.*

The *George Prince* ferry. *Courtesy of The Historic New Orleans Collection.*

The *George Prince* ferry near Morgan City, circa 1953–54. *Photograph taken by Ira Von and Mildred Walling, provided by Sue Ellen Ash.*

Soon after this author's 2006 UL–Lafayette master's thesis documentary project in communication, *The Luling Ferry Disaster*, was released, garnering considerable attention by local print and broadcast media, a memorial committee, led by St. Charles Councilman Larry Cochran, was established.

After meeting for several months, the bureau voted on the monument's appearance and future location. The Luling–Destrehan Ferry Disaster Memorial Committee included family members and friends of the deceased. St. Charles Parish Councilman Paul Hogan, an architect, created the design for the monument. This author was given the task of writing the history of the tragedy, which appeared on stations around the monument.

Today, the monument stands at the East Bank Bridge Park in Destrehan. The Pritchetts' wish came true. The *George Prince* Ferry Memorial unveiling ceremony occurred on Saturday, October 17, 2009. Iris Songy's solacing Bible verse is featured on the memorial: "When you pass through the water, I will be with you, in the rivers you shall not drown. For I am the Lord, your God, the Holy One of Israel, your Savior," (Isaiah 43:2–3).

Fred Hurt, known as "Dakota Fred" on the Discovery Channel's reality TV show *Gold Rush*, had a chilling chapter in his life prior to gold mining. Hurt was a commercial diver involved in the recovery of the victims and vehicles on the *George Prince* ferry. After all these years, Hurt still gets goosebumps when thinking of the haunting story of how he found the exact location of the crash. While searching the river in the darkness of the night for victims and vehicles, Hurt noticed a green, glowing circular light on the surface of the water. The spooky light was about two hundred to three hundred yards from the Luling ferry landing. Under Hurt's insistence, recovery efforts moved to that spot on the river. Only Hurt could see the ghostly light. There, at the deepest part of the river, which is ninety-two feet deep, they discovered the majority of the vehicles and victims.

Was the *George Prince* cursed? The ferry had another October tragedy forty-four years earlier. On Sunday, October 23, 1932, in Natchez, Mississippi, a bus filled with Black residents en route to a Baptist convention pulled into the ferry landing to get onto the *George Prince*. Because it was dark at dusk, the bus driver didn't notice that the *George Prince* had already taken off. The bus plunged into the Mississippi River. Nineteen drowned, and three were rescued.

The Continental Grain Elevator Explosion (December 22, 1977): The Deadliest Grain Dust Explosion of the Modern Era

Westwego, Louisiana, founded in 1870 by the Texas and Pacific Railroad, is a small town located on the outskirts of New Orleans on the West Bank in Jefferson Parish. No one really knows how the town got its name. Folklore tells the story of rail workers who yelled to travelers who left the Westwego train station, "West we go!" Westwego was the site from which the railroad was repaid by the state to build a railroad to the west.

In 1893, a hurricane destroyed a fishing village on Cheniere Caminada, a small barrier island west of Grand Isle. The death toll was 779. Many survivors moved their families to Westwego, as it was a safer region inland. Like most towns, tragedy encompassed some of Westwego's history, and more would arrive as the years progressed.

In December 1977, the arctic temperatures from Canada reached the United States, making it the coldest winter ever recorded in America's history. The energy crisis crippled the economy. President Jimmy Carter offered little hope. Citizens were beginning to feel boxed in.

In New Orleans, the city's transit system was millions of dollars in debt. The cultural landscape was dominated by the *Treasures of Tutankhamen* exhibit that was reigning at the New Orleans Museum of Art. It was the hottest ticket in town.

The week of December 18, 1977, began with the Saints' last game of the season. They predictably lost to the Falcons, 35–7. The Christmas season was in full swing in Terrytown, and retail had its best season to date. Schwegmann's in Gentilly had the cheapest groceries in the area. Loyola got TV's tape of the future: a video player. And *Saturday Night Fever* was featured at The Plaza in Lake Forest.

A 1963 photograph of the Continental Grain Company elevator. *Courtesy of The Historic New Orleans Collection.*

On Thursday morning, a little after 9:00 a.m., Walt Pierce had just dropped his daughter at St. John Berchmans preschool in the Sugar Hill section of Gentilly. Pierce reported:

> *Well, I just dropped my daughter off at preschool, and I'm driving east on Gentilly Boulevard, and I noticed in my rearview mirror this unusual-looking cloud. Turns out, it wasn't a cloud; it was a cloud of smoke. And as I turned around, I was able to turn around at one point, it looked like a mushroom cloud, and I said, "Something's not right. Something's definitely not right." I was a reporter for WGSO radio at the time, and I immediately got on the two-way radio and called in, and we soon found out what had happened: the terrible explosion over at the Continental Grain elevator.*

Pierce was ten air miles away from the explosion of the $100 million Continental Grain Company plant in Westwego. The blast destroyed the grain elevator and forty-eight of the seventy-three grain silos used to store soybeans, wheat and oats. Thirty-six lives were lost.

Most of the eleven survivors were located near the silos, but James Stansbury was one of those who lived through the blast inside the grain elevator itself. From his hospital bed, Stansbury spoke about his horrifying experience on the *CBS Evening News*: "I was blown through a wall, because that's the only way I could've wound up where I was. I had to go through the wall to get where I was. And I figured, well, somebody must be out there, so I started hollering, 'Please help me! Won't someone please help me?'"

Thirty years later, Stansbury, along with his daughter, Amy, and granddaughter, Savannah, revisited his amazing story of survival. Stansbury spoke of his ordeal:

> *When I went to work, I don't know what happened. All I heard was, you know like if you take a match, and you turn your oven on and then you stick your match in there and it goes "*poof*"? That's all I heard, "Poof!" and then "Boom!" And I had a ceiling beam over my leg, and I looked over here* [glancing to his right], *and the wall was gone. I could see the bottom of the bin; the grain elevator bin was busted, and the grain was falling out of there, about two thousand bushels that I still had in the bin. I was trapped; I couldn't move. I had a ceiling beam over my legs. I couldn't get up. First thing I did, I checked to make sure I had everything* [body parts], *then*

A close-up of destroyed silos. *Courtesy of Frank Graff.*

Silos explosion. *Courtesy of Frank Graff.*

> *I thanked my god. And then I said, "Please, somebody come get me out of here!" I hollered like a hog caught in a trap, "Please somebody come get me out of here!" And that deputy come in there, and he says, "I hear you, boo, I'm coming!" And he come, and he put his hands underneath my arms and jerked on me, and he was scratching me all up because I had a ceiling beam, grain dust, part of the concrete building was all piled up, and I said, "Man, you hurting me! Don't do it thataway!" So, he looks at the chair, and he saw it was a regular old office chair, but you could break it out from under me. He broke it out from under me, and then I said, "Now, turn me loose; I'm all right; I can walk." And I walked out by the railroad track. There was an ambulance waiting for me, and I jumped in that, and they brought me to the hospital.*

Stansbury's testimony revealed another disturbing image: one of a body being discovered during search and rescue. He described the sight: "The guy upstairs would call me on the phone and tell me what to put on the belt. When they found him, he had the phone in his hand!"

Anger is never far from Stansbury, when thinking of the days immediately after the explosion. According to him, the plant never shut down completely: "What blew up was where they store the grain. They never even slowed down, I don't believe. They kept right on going, man, loading them ships! Money. Money honey."

A consensus on the cause of the explosion has never been reached. Stansbury recalls many incidents prior to the explosion that raise questions: "We had bomb threats three or four times a week before that, and it never did explode. I mean, a bomb threat's a bomb threat, but nothing happened. What the hell is it? It's just a threat!"

Lamentably, Stansbury passed away in 2016. He was an active member of the Council on Aging chapter in Gretna, where he volunteered, delivering food to twenty homes a day, and he also offered transportation to the elderly in his community.

Stansbury visited the grain elevator with this author in 2007, and he shared his haunting memories with production supervisor Eugene Hill. Both visited a plaque on the site that memorializes the thirty-six who died that morning. With the memory of the tragedy still lingering in the background, Stansbury reflected again with a philosophical perspective on how lucky he had been in his lifetime. His final statement at the end of his interview left this author speechless:

> *I'm totally blessed. I've had cancer twice. I was shot when I bought that liquor store. You see, the money I had gotten out of the grain elevator, I bought a liquor store. A dude come in there and shot me with a .45 with hollow points. The bullet went in my arm, out my arm and in my chest. I survived that! I'm just a survivor—that's all. The good Lord don't want me! My wife says the devil's scared if I go down there, I'm gonna take over, so I ain't gonna die! But I'm goin' one of these days. I go to church every morning, where I ask the good Lord, "Please take me home." I'm ready to go home. I'm ready to die, if he could take me. That's the only way I'm gonna get out of here!*

Flowers Wilson also survived the explosion. Like Stansbury, Wilson was buried alive beneath the twisted metal. Miraculously, he maneuvered himself out of the wreckage and to the top of one of the burning silos.

Lieutenant Commander David Scott of the Coast Guard flew the helicopter mission that saved Wilson. He described the nerve-wracking rescue basket quest on *ABC News* the evening of the explosion:

> *You can see it bouncing off several pieces of that rubble when he was trying to grab it. Of course, I was trying to hold the helicopter steady in the black*

> *smoke, somewhere between fifty and one hundred feet above him. The updrafts from the heat coming off the fire made it difficult to stay in one spot. Most of the times that he was getting a hold of it, we didn't realize that he actually did, because he was only visible part of the time in the smoke.*

Finally, Wilson jumped fifteen feet to a conveyor housing. Firemen reached him then, and he was lifted off by the helicopter. Wilson's lifesaving leap was done blindly, due to the swirling black smoke and flames that engulfed him. His landing on top of a narrow conveyor housing was truly a miracle.

Wilson's faith in Christianity has made him a prosperous and giving person. His path in life has not been easy. His injuries from the explosion were two broken legs and serious burns to his face, arms and legs. He spent three months in the hospital, but his pain didn't end there. Wilson explained:

> *I went through some terrible times after the explosion. I just love people so much, and I never thought nobody would do anything to hurt me. And come to find out, it's like everybody was turning on me. I read the Bible a lot, I meditate and pray, and when God wanna bless you, he put people into your life; when he wanna protect you, he take people out of your life. I used to be around a lot of people, a very popular guy. And all of a sudden, the closer I got to God, the more people just left me, and I was alone! And I couldn't have made it if it wouldn't have been for God. My wife divorced me, all my friends left me; I had nobody. And I was like, "What is this?" Family members, who I love so dearly and would always come to my home and eat with me and stuff like that, everybody just left. And I didn't know why. I found out something else, too. When people think you're coming into a lot of money, it's a big difference.*

There were many heroes who helped with the recovery efforts. One of them was Armond Duffourc, who worked for the Jefferson Parish Sheriff's Department's emergency services. Duffourc spoke: "I was on my day off when the grain elevator happened. In fact, I was gassing up the unit right up the street up here, and I heard the explosion, and I left from there, saw the smoke and I went straight up there. In fact, I was the first unit on the scene."

Duffourc converged on the scene at the same time State Trooper Al Willumitis did. With concrete, dust and debris still falling from the sky, their heroics and goodwill shined through the danger that surrounded them. Duffourc continued:

Right: Armond Duffourc. *Author's collection.*

Below: A pit at the bottom of the silos—Duffourc rescues Stansbury. *Courtesy of Frank Graff.*

All kind of stuff was still falling from the silos from the conveyor belt coming over the levee over the river road into the grain elevator. Dust was flying everywhere, and I could hear somebody hollering, so we got out of the unit, went down to where they used to unload the grain cars—there's like a pit; they rode the railroad cars in there, and they would tilt them down in this pit and they had a little dozer that would push it back into the conveyor to bring it up into the silos. Well, the man that was working in the silo, he was caught under his desk, and they had a beam that fell across his desk, and his chair was up under the desk, and he was jammed up under there, so Al and I got the beam away from there, and we pulled him out, and then he said, "They got another man here running the dozer!" And just as we got the guy off the desk in the pit, the dozer operator, the Black man, we

> *got him out. And then we got out of there, and just as we got out of there, the whole thing caved in right where we were. So, we were lucky. The good Lord was on our side.*

Duffourc received a plaque for his actions, as well as a letter from Michel Fribourg, the chairman and chief executive of the Continental Grain Company, thanking him for his heroism.

Jefferson Parish Deputy Chief Frank Graff, Commander of the Special Operations Bureau, was the commander of the emergency rescue services at the time of the explosion. In Graff's words: "There were people who were walking around aimlessly, very confused. It was just chaos—utter chaos. There was fire still burning on top of some of the elevators. People were actually trapped on top of some of these silos. We tended to the injured and ultimately recovered the bodies over the next several days."

The memories of the tragedy still haunt Graff today. He observed:

> *The gentleman who was on the telephone, he was just distorted from the collapse of the building, the crushing of it, the stones. He was still on the telephone; he still had the phone to his ear. It was just something out of a horror movie that you would see for the special effects; it was just unbelievable the way the people were just covered and didn't have time to react to the explosion, the collapse of their building—the head house it was called, located immediately adjacent to the silos.*

Graff recalled the different officials and agencies on the scene, assisting and investigating:

> *The investigation was done by federal authorities, ATF, along with the sheriff's office. As best as I can recall, there was no criminal activity involved, and it seems that it may have been either a spontaneous combustion—it was an extremely dry day, dry time of the year—and I think one of the theories was static electricity that possibly caused that explosion.*

The effort shown by the rescuers was a testimony to the goodwill of mankind. Graff pressed further: "The officers that I worked with stood proud and did their job—worked many, many, many hours. We had to tell a number of them to go home, because they wanted to stay there, hoping they would be able to find people that were trapped and get them out of the rubble, but no such luck—no such luck."

Left: Destroyed, tilted silos. *Courtesy of Frank Graff.*

Below: A close-up of cracked silos and pits. *Courtesy of Frank Graff.*

A close-up of destroyed silos. *Courtesy of Frank Graff.*

An officer on the back of a pickup truck. *Courtesy of Frank Graff.*

With the tragedy occurring only three days before Christmas, many families suffered through what should have been a joyous season. Some of the workers who died in the explosion were on their day off and were at the grain elevator that morning to pick up their Christmas turkey, a gift from the company.

Vivian Collins lost her husband, Alfred, in the explosion. His remains were found on New Year's Eve. He was fifty years old and had three children. Vivian reflected back on that Christmas season with sadness:

> *Usually, I'm a person around that time of the year baking homemade cakes for the holidays. I was preparing to start my baking, and one of the ladies' husbands called me and said, "Did you know that Continental Grain Company had blown up?" And I told her no because I wasn't watching the TV, and she said, "Well, turn your TV on, because Continental just blew up! My husband is going to see if your husband is all right because he just came from there; he just got off." My husband was just going on. I turned the TV on, and all I could see was smoke. I went into a frenzy, into a rage, and I just screamed and screamed! All I did was hold myself and scream and scream! I didn't know anything else to do, and I heard her say, "I'll*

Silos smoking with a train car in the forefront. *Courtesy of Frank Graff.*

> *hang up the phone. I'm coming to see about you." She came, and people began to come to sit and to see if I was okay. It was a horrible, horrible time, when all you could hear were people talking on the TV, the reporters, the smoke.*

Vivian's last, unforeseen goodbye to Alfred happened only a few minutes before the explosion. Their conversation remains fresh in her mind today:

> *At that time, my husband had just called me and asked me did I call the garage door people, because he wanted to put an automatic garage door on the house, and I told him, "Yes, I did." He called me at a quarter to nine, and he said, "Well, give me the number. Let me check them out for myself." So, I said, "Oh, so you don't trust me? OK, let me get the number for you." So, I went and got the telephone book and gave him the number, and he asked me was I OK. I told him, "Yeah, I'm OK." And he asked me, "Is the children OK?" And I said "Yes, they OK." He said, "Is the baby OK?" I said, "Why are you asking me if everybody's OK? Yeah, she OK!" And so, he said, "These guys down here are picking on me saying I'm so henpecked, all I do is call home and check in on my wife! I'll call you back the next break I get." And I said, "OK." So, he hung up, and five minutes after, that's when I was getting the call, and it was so hard because when you just talked to a person, and then the next thing you know, that person maybe's gone out of your life. It was a startling time, and I wouldn't want anybody to go through it, but people go through it every day, when something so suddenly happens.*
>
> *Later on, they came and told me to get a shower and let's go down so we can identify the body, and I did. When I got on the levee, I remember two of his cousins was holding me under the arm, and I fell. They held me back up and said, "You'll have to make it." And I went inside the Red Cross, where they was giving all of the identification. I heard the people screaming and crying, and at that point, I had braced up; I weren't crying, and all I did was gave them the information that they wanted, and I told them to take me out; I didn't want to hear the people cries. So, I gave the information and we came back home. It was five days before they found his body.*
>
> *I remember that week—and I would say a whole month—I often wondered where did the tears come from, because there was a continuous flow of tears when I would pick up his clothes to clean out the closets. Immediately, within like a week or two, I started cleaning out; I didn't want to hold on like some people want to hold on, and don't want to let go. I began to start early after I buried him.*

> *Alfred was a person that loved laughter. He was a hardworking man. I don't remember him missing a day of work. He wanted to give his wife the best. He worked hard to give his wife the best, his children the best. We were happy. We had some happy times together.*

Collins remained a widow for eighteen and a half years. She met her second husband, Courtney, at church. Sadly, he passed away in his sleep in 2009. Like Flowers Wilson, faith in God has guided Collins out of the valley of tears. She asserted:

> *My faith has increased. At that time, I didn't know what I do now. I love to reach out to women that are going through a very hard, tragic time. Matter of fact, that is what I'm doing right now. I reach out to women that have lost their son to prison or to* [a] *gun or their husband or spouse to let them know don't give up! Lots of people wants to give up; they wanna to turn to drugs or alcohol, and I would like to talk to them and let them know there's a better way.*

The Continental Grain elevator explosion. *Illustration by Eric Anderson.*

Collins published an inspirational novel in 2019 titled *Why Not a Woman?* Not letting your fears hold you back and knowing God has a plan in your life are its key takeaway messages.

Westwego had never witnessed a calamity of this magnitude before. Shirley Bourgeois had three brothers who worked at Continental; she lost two of them in the explosion, Jay and Jerry. Jerry was an avid LSU fan who'd take regular bus trips with fans to Tiger Stadium.

Bourgeois recalled that terrible and very cold morning clearly. Her race to the elevator to check on her brothers is still vivid in her memory:

> *We're driving, and they had a lady running. We picked her up, and she gave me a pair of prayer beads. She said, "Do you say the rosary?" And I said, "Yes ma'am, I do." She then said, "Well, you better say it now." I still have her rosary. When we turned around that little curve, because we couldn't see the grain elevator from where we were at, then I saw it was like a war zone. It was unbelievable.*

Nothing could prepare her for the next sight. It seemed almost incomprehensible. She continued:

> *I got out, and I started running up the levee. Norman Robinson met me, and as I was running, I looked on the side of the street, and they had a bunch of hearses. "Why are the hearses here? That's so morbid! That's for dead people!" Not realizing that they were there to pick up bodies, and I never knew that. I just didn't realize they were there to pick up my brothers. It was devastating; it really was. I hope no one ever goes through that; it's heartbreaking. And when it happens, part of you is gone, and that's part of you you'll never get back. I loved my brothers, and I also loved a lot of the guys that worked there because it was a close family, and everyone knew one another. If they had a party, they were at the parties. It was just a big, happy family there.*

Elaine Gonzales was the wife of the youngest surviving brother, Ramos. She painfully reflected: "There's so many deaths, so many funerals we had to make. So much was lost in this explosion—so many lives, so many loved ones, all at one time, no break. No break in between."

Attorney Leonard Washofsky represented Alfred Collins and one other worker who was on shift at the time. Eventually, seven lawyers, including Washofsky, banded together and formed the plaintiffs' committee. A settlement of over $25 million was reached. Speaking from his light-blue Metairie office, immersed in natural light, he discussed the focal points of the case:

> *We were able to maneuver the situation in various ways to where there was a whole list of people who were brought into the litigation, primarily contractors, even architectural firms that had designed the elevator, those that designed and sold the dust protection system and others. They were all made a part of the complex federal litigation that we filed in the Eastern District of Louisiana, the New Orleans federal court, that went on for almost two and a half years.*
>
> *No one was ever found liable, and I don't think we'll ever really know what occurred precisely, but the best guess—what our evidence led us to believe—was that dust was allowed to accumulate in closed places, and there must have been some spark of ignition. Now, we don't think anyone would light up a cigarette in that whole area. It could be machinery that sparked. We'll never really know. There was no hard evidence as to what really occurred to cause that explosion.*
>
> *The thing that shocked us as attorneys, not knowing the physics of it, was how volatile grain dust is. We learned early on that grain dust is about ten times as explosive as coal dust under the proper environment and circumstances. So, it was, in many ways, a tragedy waiting to occur. Continental Grain rebuilt that elevator afterwards and changed the whole design. Before then, it was a sort of vertical thing. There were silos vertically, and the grain would be moved from one to another and ultimately to the ships that came in from the export to the ships. Now, they do it horizontally, so they keep the flow on a much lower basis and on a more horizontal rather than a vertical basis.*
>
> *It was a feeling that we were doing a service to all these families that suffered so much, and as a result of what we were able to uncover, it certainly was a progress in rebuilding the elevators, and I think others have followed that lead to make it a much safer workplace than it was in those days.*

Because of this disaster, safety regulations in grain elevators have substantially improved in the United States and abroad. Hundreds of heat sensors are now placed inside grain elevators, so if a machine overheats, the workers are alerted immediately. Machines now shut down automatically if excessive overheating is detected. As a preventative measure, head houses, where grain is stored, have been moved to remote locations, so if an explosion occurs, the structures will not fall directly on top of the offices and control room—as they did at Continental Grain in 1977.

4

A NEW DECADE, ANOTHER MAJOR TRAGEDY

Pan Am Flight 759 (July 9, 1982): The Worst Commercial Aircraft Crash in Louisiana History

Kenner, Louisiana, is a quaint, suburban town of New Orleans, located in Jefferson Parish. The city displays a rich history. René-Robert Cavelier, Sieur de La Salle, landed here in 1682, making this the first area in the New Orleans metropolitan area where Europeans set foot. The first heavyweight boxing championship fight was held in Kenner in 1870, and a tangible piece of New Orleans antiquity, the top of the Zephyr roller coaster at Pontchartrain Beach, is on display at Veterans Memorial Park.

Kenner's New Orleans International Airport was named in honor of pioneer aviator John B. Moisant, whose parents were French Canadians. In 1910, Moisant was killed in an airplane crash in Kenner. The airport was built on the land where the crash occurred. Through the years, other great tragedies would befall here—on what some call cursed ground.

The summer of 1982 was a season of economic despair. The national unemployment average was staggering, and it reflected prominently in the New Orleans area. In the sports arena, a federal grand jury was investigating alleged widespread cocaine use among Saints players. Lloyd Price, a Kenner native and Rock & Roll Hall of Fame inductee, had recently released his seventh album, collaborating with the eccentric pianist James

The Pan Am jet *Clipper Defiance* (N4737) in San Diego two months before the crash. *Courtesy of Clint Groves, ATP, www.AirlineFan.com.*

Booker, the teacher of Harry Connick Jr. Kids were wearing Muppet shoes and watching Tom Foote on WGNO and *The Smurfs* on NBC. Video game consoles, like Intellivision, were very popular. The Warehouse District was preparing to be revamped in conjunction with the upcoming World's Fair and the booming business district. The Elmwood Plantation, the oldest home in the Mississippi Valley, was abandoned and decaying; a committee made up of preservationists, historical society leaders, politicians and others was trying to purchase its charred ruins to restore them. Its Doric columns were still standing, like unsealed treasures fading from the public consciousness.

The jubilant noise of the Fourth of July arrived on a Sunday. The fireworks at Pontchartrain Beach took the spotlight. Uncle Sam visited triplets at Baptist Hospital, while the Statue of Liberty was literally crumbling. The Space Shuttle *Columbia* landed at Edwards Air Force Base in California, Jimmy Connors defeated John McEnroe for the Wimbledon Crown and *ET* was featured at the Lakeside Theatre.

On Wednesday, afternoon thunderstorms left eight hundred Uptown residents without electricity. The forecast for the remainder of the week called for partly cloudy skies and scattered thunderstorms.

Al Hamauei, the vice-president and commercial relationship manager of First Bank and Trust in Covington, made the most important decision of his life that Friday. The following is his fated account, in his own words:

> *We were having dinner at Sal and Judy's restaurant with Sal Impastato, his wife, Judy, and C.J. and Judy Dunaway. C.J. said he was going to Las Vegas on Friday afternoon, and the guy he was gonna go with cancelled. And he said, "Do you want to go?" and I said, "Nah, I'm not a big flyer, and I've got too much work to do the next day." I was a real estate broker and appraiser at the time. Well, after spending a couple of hours with friends and having a good time, he changed my mind. He said, "Look, I guarantee you, we're gonna see Ann-Margret the next night in Las Vegas; you're gonna love it! We got front row seats; it's gonna be great!" So, I said, "OK, I'll go. No problem." The next day, I got up. I started to do some work; I was trying to get things done, trying to get ready to go, and it just got hectic, and I just started thinking about it. I just don't want to do this, but I've committed; I guess I'll go. As the day went on, something kept telling me: "You don't need to go. You don't want to go. Don't do it." I don't know what it was. God, I'm sure, was saying, "Don't do it." By about midday, I called him up and I said, "Look, I don't feel good. I don't feel like going. I've got too much to do." And he said, "I knew you'd chicken out. You don't like to fly." I said, "No, I just got this feeling I don't want to go. Are you gonna go?" He said, "No, if nobody's gonna go with me, I've got a friend who can go on Saturday or Sunday. I've got time off then. I'll go then. I'll cancel the reservations and just go another day." I had went home to do something. My wife was home, and just as I walked into the door, she was watching TV, and the crash had happened. She said, "Is that the flight you were supposed to be on?" I said, "I'm not really sure. I don't know the exact time, what we were gonna do, but I know it was this afternoon, Las Vegas, probably a lot of flights to Las Vegas, can't be the same one!" So, I called C.J. up and I said, "Turn your TV on and see what's going on!" So, he turned it on, and I said, "Is that the flight?" And he said, "Yeah, that's the flight we were supposed to be on!" This unbelievable feeling comes over you, the typical thing, you see people go on at the last minute, people get off at the last minute. We were just blessed not to go. It wasn't our time. It was just a terrible, terrible thing—the tragedy, the people that were killed. It was just horrible.*

An aerial view of the crash scene—a scar of death and destruction in the Roosevelt subdivision. *Courtesy of the Jefferson Parish Sheriff's Office.*

Pan Am World Airways Flight 759, originating in Miami and destined for Las Vegas and San Diego, crashed under heavy thunderstorms at 4:11 p.m., about one minute after taking off. The plane slammed into a Kenner neighborhood about a half mile from the end of the runway. All 137 passengers, the crew of 7, a maintenance man and 8 on the ground (6 of whom were children) were killed. Victims from twenty-three countries were aboard; it was a tragedy felt around the world.

Evelyn Pourciau bore witness to a terrifying sight she and her Roosevelt subdivision will never forget. Evelyn observed:

> *When I came out here, I was brushing on my two dogs. I could hear the trees cracking, and the plane was sputtering, like it couldn't get the motor revved up. I guess he was gunning it. It was just confusion, and when I looked up and heard the trees back here and the plane, I knew something was wrong. I was at the end of my patio, and I looked up and saw this huge piece of metal. I didn't realize it was that close to me, but then I realized the plane was falling, and it was on the left side.*

Evelyn's sister-in-law, Ruth, lived next door. The path of the plane's descent went directly through her property. Evelyn continued:

> *It was falling. Before it hit, it went through her oak tree. It had two prongs to it. It split through that tree. Can you believe this? You know how big those wings are. The wing went right through that tree and knocked half of it off, and the other half is still standing. Unbelievable. And it made a trench in her yard in the dirt. It was just inches from my sister-in-law's carport.*

> *The wing hit the street out here, which emptied all that fuel, and then the plane slid for two blocks; that's where the fuselage broke loose and went into another house right there on Hudson Street. The plane itself slid and was scattering bodies and people as it was going. It didn't land at all as a plane would land. It just exploded as it was going through. People were found still in their seats, but they all died. And I've heard since then that plane crashes, if it wouldn't be for the fire, that people would survive the crash, but the fire is what makes people die, and that's what happened here—the fire.*

Evelyn came to the aid of her neighbor across the street, whose home was struck by the plane. With pain in her eyes, she reflected:

> *I had my two grandkids here, and by the time I got through the house, everything…it looked like Hades had turned loose: the smoke, the fire, the wind, the rain! Barbara and the two kids came out on the ground, and it was sad, because she had a T-shirt on and jeans. The T-shirt just had a string across her; all of her clothes had burned off. You know I never seen skin burned, but it was like a sheet of wax coming down, and it was the most hideous thing. So, I got them and brought them over here on the swing and got some sheets out of my house, wet them, and I put them around them until the ambulance came, and the ambulance driver said that was the best thing I could've done was put wet sheets around them because if it would've been dry, it would've taken all the skin completely off.*
>
> *I got subpoena after subpoena because I was the one that saw the plane crash, and their question was, "Do you think the people on there knew they were dying?" Well, of course they knew they were dying! They'd just taken off, and when you get in this position in a plane* [gesticulating with her hands that the plane turned on its left side], *you know something's happening! So, of course they knew they were dying!*

Mike Scardino, chapter president of the Christian Motorcyclists Association, recalls his chance encounter that horrible afternoon:

> *I was coming home from work, on the corner of West Metairie and Williams Boulevard, and stopped at a red light, looked up and seen a 727 come across right in from of my windshield, about fifty feet off the ground, right above the power lines, and I said to myself, "My God, that plane is low!" When I said that, the plane took a left bank turn and tilted its wing, like it was trying to get off the neighborhood. All of a sudden, it started raining, I didn't see it no*

The Schultz home at 1624 Fairway was one of fifteen houses destroyed or damaged. Evelyn assisted her neighbors as best she could. *Courtesy of Dr. John Baye.*

more, and he went into the rain. I heard a shaking boom explosion. About a two-hundred-foot mushroom cloud went up in the air right there, and I said, "Oh my Lord! The plane just crashed in the neighborhood!" I happen to be coming to work on 17th Street and Roosevelt at a friend of mine's house that day, putting up a canopy for him. When I got here, as it happened, I pulled up, and a friend of mine jumped out of his house and said that a house just blew up in his backyard, and I said, "No, a 727 just crashed in your backyard!" He couldn't believe me, so we walked into the site, went down 17th Street, over to Taylor to Hudson Street. All of the houses were leveled where the plane's path went through. Things were on fire, burning. There was a car parked in the driveway, and it blew up right next to us, so we decided we couldn't do anybody any good because nobody was out. We got out of there, and it started raining like I never seen it rain before! If it wouldn't have rained that hard, I believe it would've still been on fire right now. The plane was laying on top of a house a few houses over from the corner of 17th and Taylor. Explosions. Fire engines started coming. That's when CB radios were big then; I got on the REACT and got on channel 16 and told them that a plane had crashed in a backyard neighborhood on 17th and Roosevelt. They kind of didn't believe me at first. I kept telling them, and then all the police started coming, ambulances and fire trucks. We just backed off from the scene and stood around and watched the firemen go to work.

That night, I left, and I came back, and people were working on a house right across the street from where I was working at. They set up a makeshift morgue there, bringing the bodies out of the plane, into the house, right under the carport. I went home, got some friends together and brought food back for the workers that were working there through my Lion's Club. They brought a young man out with just his torso showing. They brought a young boy out, burnt, just as stiff as could be. At that time, when I seen the body, it was about ten or eleven o'clock at night, I had been here all evening, and I decided to just go home and get out the way after I seen those bodies. It's just something I'd never forget.

Investigators determined that a vortex of wind, a windshear, pushed the plane downward, causing the crash. *Illustration by Eric Anderson.*

Led by Patricia Goldman, Vice Chairman of the National Transportation Safety Board, federal investigators concluded windshear (a sudden change of wind speed and direction) and the plane's full load of passengers and fuel combined to cause the accident. The windshear sensor on the western edge of the airport was not functioning; vandals had damaged it with gunfire.

The jet encountered a very powerful windshear called a microburst, causing it to lose altitude and plunging downward. The plane initially hit a tree on Williams Boulevard before plowing through four blocks of the Roosevelt subdivision. Pan Am Flight 759 was the third weather-related commercial aircraft crash in the United States that year.

Mark Larkin was a civil defense worker at the scene of the accident. Mark observed:

> *Civil defense no longer exists in most areas of the country. It was replaced in the 1980s by FEMA. It was the local civil defense people who were supposed to go into action and start doing the rescues, maintaining order, doing whatever was necessary until the other authorities, National Guard or military, were sent in to take over.*

You had all sorts of rescue personnel showing up from the hospitals, the sheriff's office, the fire department, you had people coming in from surrounding jurisdictions: St. Charles, Kenner, New Orleans, all coming in to assist, and it took a little while to get a command structure together to organize everybody and see what was going on.

The end of the path of the plane was just a pile of debris that was probably as tall as a two-story house with the tail section of the aircraft on top of it, and that was the only thing I saw that, at a glance, would've indicated that it was a plane crash. You had the very tail end of the fuselage and the control surfaces with the big Pan Am logo on it, and that was it. I didn't see another fragment of an airplane around that was big enough to identify, at a glance, as a large aircraft. There were all sorts of debris scattered everywhere: trees knocked down, houses destroyed, clothes from the homes and from the aircraft. There were bodies and pieces of bodies all over the place: in the street, in yards, in trees, piled on top of one another. Many of them had their clothes burned off. At one point, once the fires got out, I remember looking down at the gutters, and what had been previously running with burning jet fuel was now running with blood.

The rest of that evening, in fact, for the next couple of days, it was just body recovery, body part recovery. They had a refrigerated tractor-trailer that

A destroyed house with a doll in rubble. *Courtesy of* The Times-Picayune.

The vertical stabilizer of the jet being lifted and removed from the neighborhood. *Courtesy of Dr. John Baye.*

> *was backed in on one of the side streets that the bodies were being put in as they were picked up. Some were being put in garages of houses until this refrigerated truck showed up to be used as a temporary morgue.*
>
> *As time went on, the number of people working on it diminished, because as one might imagine, it was in July, and most of the bodies and large parts of bodies were recovered the same evening and eventually put in this refrigerated truck, but for the next couple of days, you were having to go through the rubble, through the trees and everything, looking for smaller parts that had been missed the evening of the ninth. You also had all of the food that was in the refrigerators of these houses that were destroyed putrefying in the heat, so the longer it went, the worse it smelled and the fewer people you found out there fooling with it. My friend and I that rolled out there the evening of the ninth were still out there three days later. That was when we left.*

The rescue of the miracle baby was of special importance to Mark. He added:

> *I was in the yard area of the same house, as was a couple of firemen. Deputy Hibbs thought he saw something moving on the ground and that he thought he heard a sound; threw over a mattress, and there was Melissa Trahan, sixteen to eighteen months old, on the ground, under this mattress and debris. The assumption was that she was in a crib or lying on a bed, and when the plane came through, it actually just flipped it over, and the mattress and this other stuff fell on top of her and protected her and saved her from the fire that would have been around for a time before it was put out. Deputy Hibbs picked her up; she was put in an ambulance and taken to the hospital and turned out to be in really good shape. It was an elating moment because everybody's spirits were really low; we figured this was*

> *going to be strictly body recovery, and to find even one survivor, particularly a small child like that, really boosted the spirits of everybody because that was beyond all expectation at that point to find somebody alive.*

Nick Congemi, former Kenner and Causeway Police Chief, shared his discourse and personal experiences related to the catastrophe:

> *I was working for the Kenner Police Department and also Pan American Airways at the time. In this particular situation, I was actually working for the airlines out at the airport when the flight took off, and as soon as I found out what had taken place, I rushed to the scene and assumed my responsibilities as a police officer for the city of Kenner for twelve years at that time. I was a lieutenant, and I was designated as the on-scene commander, control and everything that the police department did, although it was a great collaborative and team effort of many, many agencies that were involved from the federal government, state, National Guard, state police, Jefferson Parish Sheriff's Office, New Orleans, the New Orleans Coroner's Office, FBI. There were many agencies involved, but I had responsibility for the Kenner Police Department itself.*
>
> *When you walk through something like that, it gives you a good idea of what it looks like to walk through Hell, with flames all around you and people yelling, screaming. It was a lot of confusion, and it took quite a bit of effort to bring things under control and into an orderly fashion.*
>
> *In order to process the crime scene, as we call it in law enforcement—and that's the way that we handled it—everything had to be charted, measured and accounted for. All of those passengers, as well as people on the ground, were accounted for in those small, very tiny parts, like fingers and teeth and ears were spread all over the ground. It's something really hard to imagine, and it's very difficult for the average person to even fathom how something like that could happen. There was a section of the nose of the aircraft that was left intact, and even within that, the bodies were packed so tight in that front compartment that you couldn't distinguish them from each other.*
>
> *We worked for some twenty-four to thirty-six hours without any rest at all. And to think, in my mind, we were working to cleanse the city of what had invaded our quiet, sleepy town that we knew and loved. It was like a blemish, even though I know that is a harsh word to be for these circumstances, but it was something that we had to clean up, erase, and move out of the way in order for us to get on with our lives. I think it took seven to ten days to get everything cleared. I know some people that still have*

thoughts and dreams about what they saw there. Some of them say that they will never get over it, and I can understand that.

I don't think I've ever seen a greater spirit of cooperation amongst not only the many agencies involved but also the community and the residents who lived in that area who probably had the same feelings that I did: we had to get this cleared up as quickly as possible. People came out; they offered assistance to all of the personnel that were there, whether it be state, local or federal. You saw these people that were cooking for us; they were certainly treating it as a typical Louisiana event, where they all come out as a community and as a family and want to help. Some of these people were not capable, nor did they want to pick up body parts, but they were able to cook, they were able to provide water, they were able to give us some distraction from the grisly task at hand.

An NTSB spokesman said that the control tower had warned the pilot. Well, they didn't warn the pilot; they advised him. If they knew what they professed to know, they should've not allowed the take off. The FAA and the NTSB, they ultimately control those things, so I thought that was a horrible thing for them to say to try to besmirch the integrity of the flight crew.

Congemi's assertion was supported by Louisiana Senator J. Bennett Johnston in a 1982 interview with WDSU reporter Mark Phillips. Johnston stated:

Clearly, we've had enough warning from enough accidents involving windshear that we should have acted as a nation a long time ago. There are both devices, both on board the plane and to be used on the ground, that can be employed that are not being fully employed, and there are steps you can take, the controllers and the tower can take, to abort landings or to stop takeoffs when the proper warnings come.

Captain Kenneth L. McCullers and copilot Donald G. Pierce are pillars of selflessness in Congemi's heart. Congemi remarked:

I didn't learn 'till some years later of what true heroes they were. They knew they were going to crash and—probably one of the most courageous things that you could ever think of that a person would do—the captain tried to steer that plane towards a canal, which was maybe two blocks away, to lessen the impact on a residential neighborhood, so when the left wing dipped, probably very erratically, it may not have been the total fault of the windshear. It was the captain and the copilot who knew they were

> *going down and tried to lessen the impact on a residential neighborhood. They couldn't save themselves; that was totally out of the question. They knew being that close to the ground that they were not going to survive, but in spite of that, within those very few seconds that they knew that they were going to die, they tried to save others, which I thought was the most courageous act that any human being could do.*

Former Kenner Fire Chief D.J. Mumphrey oversaw putting out the flames urgently after the crash. An active member of the Elmwood Fitness Center, Mumphrey assessed his involvement with the tragedy from the gym's outdoor pool deck:

> *The fire service, when we responded with four engines at first, called for mutual aid and then basically surrounded the scene. The first order of business was actually get the fire out. That operation lasted about two hours; the fire was completely put out. We had fire service from Jefferson Parish, Harahan. The airport sent their foam units from the airport to cover the entire area after we extinguished most of the fire. There was a lot of work to be done the rest of those days there. We spent about four days just in the removal process. We thought we did well, and I had to ask myself that a few times. I actually sought help from a friend of mine. He was a Baptist minister but also a fire chief named Terry Hayes at the time from Shreveport. I had gotten to know Terry as a young firefighter with the LSU fire training school; I always admired the way he handled things. After every incident like this, regardless of how anyone feels, always bring in some psychological help, find a friend, somebody you can talk to, because as much as you think you've got your act together, there is something about that much devastation or trauma to the brain*

The Pan Am crash site and first responders. *Courtesy of Dr. John Baye.*

cells that you ought to at least be given the opportunity to talk about if you feel there's any side effects or any doubts in your mind.

My lesson learned is to make sure that when you're setting up a command post that you make sure you have someone to handle the press and make sure that you're giving them accurate information, as much information as you could possibly give them, but keep them as corralled as possible, and you control the media output. We didn't do that.

Dr. Robert Barsley, President of the American Academy of Forensic Sciences, was assigned to help identify people killed in Pan Am Flight 759; it was his first week working as a forensic dentist. The following is Dr. Barsley's personal remembrance in his own poignant words:

Over the course of that week or six days, we examined every body bag that had dental remains in it and made a chart of those findings of what types of fillings those individuals had in their mouth. We took X-rays of the individuals' mouths, the remains that we had, and the airline, working through their manifest of passengers, brought to us the dental records from the victims. There were people from twenty-three different countries on the airplane. We received dental records on the vast majority of them, and we were able to identify through dental methods about 70 percent of the crash victims.

A gentleman I knew and his wife were on the airplane. As it turns out, the very first body bag that was opened up that I attended was actually this gentleman's wife. We were able to make a dental identification based on the findings in her mouth very rapidly. During the course of the week, I spent, personally, much time looking for the remains of the husband. As it turns out, his body was so badly damaged that we were really never able to recover much in the way of dental remains, and he was identified through fingerprints and through other methods.

Dr. John Baye lost his six-year-old daughter, Lisa, in the crash. She had two older siblings, Jacques and Stephanie. In Dr. Baye's words:

She was the light of our life, always excited. She was involved in the little children's group at church; she was in a musical the Christmas before. They sang and had a little play that they put on. She was good with putting things together, little art projects and good at matching colors. I think she would have probably ended up being an artist had she lived and grown to be an adult.

> *Years ago, while working my way through school, I was in the plumbing business. I ran my own little business. Every day, when I would come home, she would be waiting for me in the evening. We had a storm door on the front of our house, and she knew about what time I would come home, and she would be waiting by the front door. The minute she would see my truck pull in, she'd holler. I'd have the window down, and I could hear her, "Daddy's home! Daddy's home!" I'd come in and go right away to take a shower, and she would stand outside my bathroom door and talk to me the whole time I was in the shower. She'd be going a mile a minute, telling me what happened that day, what she did, what she wanted to do, what she wanted me to get for her and just a real great little personality. She never met a stranger; everybody was her friend and* [she] *just loved to talk.*
>
> *It was July the 9th, 1982, and I got up that morning. I was plumbing a house on State Street; the house was being renovated, and it was four feet off the ground. The day before, my son wanted to come to work with us, so he came to work. He played under there all day while I worked. Well, Lisa had asked if she could come the next day, which was the 9th, and I had this thing about little girls getting dirty. I didn't want her playing in the dirt and getting dirty, and I didn't know if I would be able to keep an eye on her. My son was a little bit older. So, that morning, I got up and I'd always kiss them goodbye. Well, I went into the bedroom, and I went to kiss her, and I thought, "Well, I don't want to wake her up because she's gonna want to come with me." So, I blew her a kiss, and I left and went to work.*

Morning turned to afternoon. Dr. Baye continued:

> *I told my wife I'd be home around 3:00, and she had a doctor's appointment, so she left to go to the doctor's appointment, and Lisa went to play at the Schultz's, and the two bigger kids were home by themselves. My daughter Stephanie was twelve then and Jacques was ten. I got in at about 3:45; I ran a little later than I thought, and I came in, checked on the kids, saw what they were doing, found out where Lisa was, and then I was going to take a shower to get ready to go. There was going to be a wake that night for my uncle, and I was gonna go to the wake. I called just before I went into the shower and spoke to Lisa to see if she wanted to come home then; I was gonna go get her, and she said, "No, Miss Schultz is gonna go take us to get a snowball, so can I come after we get the snowballs?" I said, "Sure." So, I hung up the phone, went into the bathroom, was just getting ready to get into the shower when there was this like earthquake. The house*

Lisa Baye. *Courtesy of Dr. John Baye.*

> *shook, and there was a rumbling. I heard this loud, muffled explosion. My bathroom was in a hallway that, as you opened it, if you looked on angle, you could look out into my den and look out the window. My wife had her plants hanging in the window; there were no drapes there. When I looked out of the window, all I could see was fire everywhere. I ran to check on Jacques and Stephanie, and they were OK. I heard the neighbor in the back screaming. She was hysterical. She had just had a baby, and her house had been hit. I ran back and got in the backyard, and I helped her and her baby and her son. I got them over the fence to try and get them out of the neighborhood. I came back and took a quick inventory. We had a little dog; I got the dog. And I thought, "OK, I have Jacques. I have Stephanie. Oh my God! Where's Lisa?" Stephanie said she's at the Schultz's. And I said, "I need to go get her!" The lady and an elderly lady that I'd gotten into my vehicle also to help her get out the neighborhood started screaming, "No! You gotta get us out of the neighborhood!" Everything was on fire, and there was a four-inch gas main that the plane, when it slid, it had dug out the ground. It was turned up, and it was shooting this flame of gas into the air, and the fire department was afraid that it might explode. So, they were telling everybody you had to leave. Against my better judgment, I got everybody out, and for some reason, I felt that I needed to call my grandmother. I called her, and she said, "Johnny, are y'all okay?" And I said, "Yeah, I'm so worried about Lisa; I have to go back!" And she said, "Oh, Lisa's at the hospital. They just said on the news she's at East Jefferson Hospital." So, I hung up the phone, and I headed for East Jefferson.*

An old Catholic priest at East Jefferson who knew Dr. Baye from previous tragedies—two of Dr. Baye's brothers had been killed—greeted him as soon as he entered, wanting to talk. Dr. Baye understood that whenever you saw him, it was bad news. A lot of commotion soon arose as Deborah, Dr. Baye's wife, rushed in. The father informed them that Lisa was burned over 95 percent of her body and was in surgery. Deborah fainted. Medics wanted to put her into a hospital room, but when she was revived, the Bayes declined. A room on the third floor was prepared for them to wait while Lisa underwent a four-and-a-half-hour surgery. When the Bayes entered the waiting room, over three hundred members of their church were gathered there for prayers and support. They stayed with them throughout the night. The surgeon was Dr. Gustavo Colón, whom Deborah just had an appointment with earlier. Before the surgery, Lisa kept crying for her mommy and daddy. Dr. Colón held her and told her it would be OK and that she'd see her mom and dad after a while. After the surgery, Lisa was brought to the ICU, where her parents could soon visit her. Dr. Colón alerted them of how bad it was; seeing Lisa like this would be a difficult thing. In Dr. Baye's words:

> *When we went into the room, it was horrendous. Our beautiful little girl was burned beyond recognition, and she was just suffering so much. She was in agony, and her whole body was trembling. Her eyes were swollen shut, and her lips were swollen, extremely large. So, we went over and got on either side of the bed. We leaned over and whispered and said, "Lisa, it's Mom and Dad," and when we did, she started to try to like sit up. We told her to just wait. She was going to be OK and that we were going to place her in Jesus's hands. We began to pray for her, and while we were praying for her, she began to get much worse. The doctors ran and said, "Okay you're gonna have to go. We need to work on her." We went back out into the waiting area, and about an hour later, the doctor came out and said, "If you wanna see her, now's the time." I knew it was awful, and I actually went out in the stairwell at East Jefferson alone and just prayed that God would stop her suffering, even if it meant her not living anymore because I couldn't bear to see her suffer that way. About twenty minutes later, the doctor said, "You can go in and see her." We went in, and we saw her for the last time. While we were in there, she began to go into cardiac arrest, so they made us get out. It's been a while, but I think it was around eleven o'clock that night, our six-and-a-half-year-old daughter died of cardiac arrest. Her heart gave out due to the trauma to her little body from all the burns and injuries she incurred from the plane crash.*
>
> *I have no fear of death. I believe with all my heart and every fiber of my being that when I close my eyes on this side of eternity, I'll open them in the presence of my God and King. I believe the first thing I'll hear is, "Daddy's home!" I have a daughter who's waiting for me and a son.*

(This interview with Dr. Baye was conducted on January 17, 2012. Jacques passed away on January 19, 2006. Stephanie passed away on June 11, 2021.)

Left: Leo Noone jumping from bushes (April 1972). *Courtesy of Mary Noone.*

Right: Mary Noone with her father and their Cessna plane in Hialeah, Florida (July 1972). *Courtesy of Mary Noone.*

"Smooth seas do not make skillful sailors," an African proverb wisely alliterates. Mary Noone has navigated the sea of sorrow, losing her father, Leo, in the crash; he was the flight engineer.

> *When I think of my dad, I think of him being very lighthearted, easy-going and having a sense of humor, even as a teenager, when you don't think your parents are really cool anymore. I remember, one time, he took my friend Sue and I to the beach with him and my mom. We'd always go up to Juno Beach, which is around Jupiter, and rent a hotel room for a weekend or something. One time, we were coming back from the beach, Sue and I had walked down there by ourselves, and as we were coming back to the hotel room, I could see my dad hiding behind some bushes, and I said to Sue, "Watch, he's gonna jump out and try to scare us." And sure enough, as we got closer, I had my camera with me, he jumped out and screamed, "Boo!" I have a picture of him doing that. It was just a funny instance as a teenager that I still appreciated my dad's humor.*
>
> *When my father died in the plane crash, my mother was part of a settlement with Pan Am. Through the research, I had decided that I wanted to adopt a little girl from China and give her a home that she probably wouldn't have otherwise. Out of the tragedy of my father dying, I was able to adopt my daughter, Jenna. I got her in 1999, and she was nine months old. Oh gosh, if my father would've known her! We talk about her grandpa, and I tell her stories about him. She always asked me, "Do you think he would've liked me?" I said, "Oh my God, yes! He would've loved you to death!"*

Bill Fagaly, a former curator of African art at the New Orleans Museum of Art, was privileged to know crash victims Steve and Marion Millendorf, independent geologists who cowrote several professional geological publications. Both were New Yorkers who made Uptown New Orleans their home. Fagaly spoke fondly of them as he sat on a park bench outside of the museum one chilly afternoon:

> *I knew the Millendorfs through the museum. They were members, and they were young collectors of contemporary art. I had a group at the time called Friends of Contemporary Art, and they were members of that group. They were a wonderful, delightful, young couple who were very enthusiastic about collecting and discovering new artists. They were just the kind of people the museum likes to work with because of their enthusiasm and thirst for knowledge. They really wanted to learn more about art in general but in what they should be doing as collectors. I really liked them both. They were very upbeat, positive people, fun to be with, intelligent. They were cool.*

Geologist Christopher Baynas was a friend of the Millendorfs. He shared an office at Explorer Oil & Gas with Steve. From the maritime-themed chamber of his stately Mandeville home, Baynas remarked:

> *They didn't have any children; they had a dog. They liked to go to Vegas; they stayed at the Riviera. The night of the accident, we were supposed to go to a Barbara Mandrell concert, the four of us: my wife, Marion, Steve and myself. He called me Thursday night and canceled out. He said they decided, spur of the moment, to go to Vegas at the Riviera. They used to stay at the Riviera all the time. They said they got the last two seats on the plane. And I said, "That's fine. Have at it."*
>
> *The next day, I was driving back from work from downtown New Orleans on the Pontchartrain Expressway and saw the smoke coming from near the airport. I turned on the radio and heard that it was a Pan Am flight nonstop to Vegas had crashed, and I didn't find out 'till the next morning that Steve and Marion were on that flight. I heard it was a microburst. It was fast. The plane didn't get very high in the air, so it came down pretty fast. There probably wasn't a lot of suffering involved. The plane had a full load of fuel on it, so it probably burned at a pretty high temperature.*
>
> *Steve was a real outgoing guy, very smart. He would have done really well if he wouldn't have passed on. He was pretty sharp. Marion, she wasn't a practicing geologist. She might have been, eventually. She was*

working with geologists doing the New Orleans Geological Society bulletin. They both were very smart, sophisticated-type people. They liked to go to nice restaurants, art collections. He collected books and was very soft-spoken, but friendly.

At the time of their deaths, Marion was thirty-seven and Steve was twenty-seven. Their legacy remains strong today. Their art collection was donated to the New Orleans Museum of Art, and the Gibbet Hill Foundation was established in their memory.

Former Jefferson Parish President Aaron Broussard was the mayor of Kenner at the time of the crash. The following are the mayor's own words about this dark chapter in his city's history:

I was in City Hall at the time, and the mayor's office was parallel to Williams Boulevard, but it had no windows. The rain began to pound on top of the roof, so we knew some ferocious storm was afoot but paid no attention to that because that comes and goes in the summers for us. But then I heard this shrieking, screaming woman from down the hall, and she was screaming that an airplane had just crashed on her house, and she ran into the mayor's office, and she was really frantic. She was trying to convey her panic to my secretary, and knowing them both, I realized something awful had happened. I said, "Where are you talking about?" She said, "Mr. Mayor, just a couple blocks away!" I jumped up, and I ran out the back of City Hall. As I'm running out to my car, the police chief, Sal Lentini, was running out of his police station, trying to get to a car. We both hopped in his car, and within a minute, we were at the air crash scene, which was very horrific. We parked right at Fairway, looking into the crash, looking eastward toward New Orleans. The amount fire with the amount of rain was causing this billowing smoke to just come rolling out, and you could not pierce visually into it. You could see the electric wires just kind of dancing in the street. You heard the hissing of what sounded like gas, and you just knew that you were looking at a surreal scene. It just didn't seem real, and out of that scene comes a woman and a small child, very horribly burned.

Logistically, we set up a pattern of recovery, where I established a grid system. We would set up a team of three, where there would be a Kenner policeman, or a Jefferson Parish policeman, and a National Guardsman, that would go to each grid section, and they would recover the different elements that were in that grid, and they would bag them appropriately based on what it is they were recovering. At one juncture early on in that pattern of trying to bring all of the evidence of that crash to another site, there was a representative of the NTSB that was there that had halted my operation while I was at a Catholic mass, honoring those that had died. I was very upset with that and approached the woman who was identified as the one who shut it down and told her how dare she shut down this process that had been initiated, and she said, "Well, I represent the NTSB, and we're in charge of this site, and this plane's not going anywhere. This is our plane." I said something to the effect, "Well, this is my city, and you need to get your plane out of my city, because I need to clean up this neighborhood! I got to restore it back to normalcy. These people should not be made to look at this horrible scene, where it would be psychologically damaging to them and the residents of this city that had to constantly live under the air traffic that was generated by that airport." I had a mission, on behalf of everyone involved and concerned, to extract everything from that site as rapidly as I could. When I had this tête-à-tête with this representative, there were cameras all around, and I basically blasted the NTSB for what I call the "Mickey Mouse Operation," the way they were coming in and interrupting what we were doing to get it under control. Later that day, a top representative of the NTSB flew in and met me on site, and we resolved those matters very quickly. The elements of the plane were removed to a certain spot at the airport, where the NTSB could do their job as long as it would take them to do their job and putting together the different clues as to what caused the crash. In reaching that compromise, the rest of the cleanup operations went fairly smoothly. Once all the items, artifacts and evidence were removed from the site, then came the part of digging out all of that contaminated soil: the fuel, the blood, everything that had mixed together as a result of the crash. We excavated, I want to say, about three feet deep to make sure that we got it. It was huge bulldozers supplied by the Louisiana National Guardsman. They scooped it up. They put it in these huge trucks; they all looked like dinosaurs, they were so big. All of that was hauled away from the site so that we could ultimately begin to put new soil back in and create a sense of stabilization to the area.

A call for help came from the West Coast. The crash of PSA Flight 182, which occurred four years earlier, remains the deadliest aircraft disaster in California history. Broussard elaborated:

I remember a call I got from the mayor of San Diego, a very kind gentleman, and he called me up and said, "Mr. Mayor, look, I hate to disturb you, I know you're very busy, but I would like to bring a group of people from San Diego who helped clear up our site; it took us five or six months to do that, and we want to come in and show you a lot of different techniques that we found out were the best way to clean the area up quicker. And I said, "Mr. Mayor, with all due respect, I've done that already. I'm planting trees."

He says, "You're planting trees? You got all of the contaminated soil? You got all the pieces of the plane out?" "Yes, sir. Yes, sir. We did." I said, "We got all of that done, and I'm planting trees there to try to create a softer atmosphere for those people who have to live and look at that site for a prolonged period of time." And I kinda joked and said, "Mr. Mayor, if you want me to create a Kenner team and bring them to San Diego, maybe I can show you some of the things that we did." It was a very generous offer, and we got offers like that from around the country because people's hearts went out.

In addition to the requirement now of putting windshear detectors at airports all over the country, the other major positive effect that that crash had was it forced a resolution of the expansion of the east–west runway at the New Orleans International Airport. There was a logjam where the airport, owned by the City of New Orleans, and Dutch Morial was the mayor at the time, trying to expand into St. Charles Parish into the marsh with land they had purchased but needed permission from the St. Charles Parish government to do so. Like any other major business that comes into a parish or a city, the government wanted to make sure that for whatever inconveniences that were being caused to their residents and constituencies that there would be some revenue stream that would come into government that could be pointed to to offset those complaints by enhancing the quality of life for their citizens. It was an absolute stalemate, because the airport wasn't owned by the state, therefore it couldn't be expropriated by the City of New Orleans. It was just stuck on stuck, and it was going nowhere! Immediately after the crash, I asked for a joint meeting with the officials from St. Charles Parish in my conference room, which they obliged. I made an appeal to them at the time. I said, "You've seen the death and carnage that this crash has rendered to my city and to those that have suffered. We need to stop planes taking off over rooftops and allow planes to take off and land over marsh. This would save lives, and it would be a great enhancement to the growth of the airport." But that appeal really fell on deaf ears at the time. It was an adamant stance of revenues, and revenues were going to be the key to permission. My administration developed an idea that I brought to St. Charles Parish, and I presented to Dutch Morial. It was simply this:

> *Kenner, in order to protect its citizens from other like crashes in the future and reduce that risk over rooftops, we would surrender the same percentage of sales tax that we collected from the airport in proportion to the amount of landmass that St. Charles Parish would allow the airport to go into their parish for. So, for instance, if the east–west runway created a landmass in the marsh that was equivalent to 10 percent of the total footprint of the airport, then Kenner would surrender 10 percent of the sales tax it collected to St. Charles Parish. That was ultimately accepted by St. Charles Parish, and then the east–west runway was built, and that was the major impetus for building that east–west runway, and it wouldn't be there today, I don't believe, if the Pan Am crash hadn't occurred.*

At the time, the crash was the second deadliest in U.S. aviation history; as of today, it remains the fifth deadliest. The disaster led to the development of sophisticated equipment that incorporates Doppler radar to predict severe downdrafts, virtually eliminating the violent weather phenomenon as a threat to airline safety. Windshear detection and alert systems were mandated by the U.S. Federal Aviation Administration for installation in all commercial aircraft by 1993.

Pan American Airlines and the federal government, facing lawsuits in excess of $3 billion, accepted blame for the jet crash in a hearing on May 13, 1983, in New Orleans and offered victims' families an undisclosed settlement. Wendell Gauthier, a lawyer representing several of the victims' families, called the move "astounding."

A memorial to the victims of Pan Am Flight 759 was constructed at Our Lady of Perpetual Help Catholic Church in Kenner, one mile from the crash site.

Once the world's largest international air carrier, Pan American World Airways, founded in 1927, ceased operations in 1991 after declaring bankruptcy.

5

THE 1990s ALMOST ESCAPED A MAJOR TRAGEDY BUT COULDN'T

Mother's Day Bus Crash on 610 (May 9, 1999): The Worst Vehicular Accident in Louisiana History

Rising out of City Park, a mysterious hill stands tall, boasting its claim as the highest point in New Orleans. Its formation is man-made, composed of leftover dirt and rubble from the construction of Interstate 610.

The 610 cuts right through City Park, home to the oldest grove of mature live oaks in the world. A 1972 lawsuit against the construction of the highway argued a 1968 law restricted the use of park land for expressways, unless there was no other alternative. The suit failed. Here, today, the 610 Stompers are a New Orleans icon, bringing smiles and charity to many. Returning the ordinary man to the glory of dance is their mission. The contemporary history of I-610 has faded from public memory, but many of its woeful chronicles remain.

The year 1999 was one to celebrate the past and fear the future in Louisiana. The first Mardi Gras celebrated its tricentennial at Iberville and Bienville's Bayou Mardi Gras in Buras. Future shock roared with the transition from pagers to cellphones, and Y2K approached like a Category 5 hurricane.

On Mother's Day morning, the Jazz Fest reveled in reverence to Al Hirt, who had died the week before. Dave Treen and David Vitter were headed for a House seat runoff. The Oakwood Mall was abuzz after Monica Lewinsky's book tour visit. Saints coach Mike Ditka had a fresh and expensive courtship with Ricky Williams. Ricky Martin topped the *Billboard* charts with "Livin' La Vida Loca," and *The Mummy* was featured at The Galleria.

That morning, attorney Russell Bergstrom was about to play some golf at City Park. Hoping for an ace, he encountered an albatross instead, changing his life forever. In Bergstrom's words:

> *City Park has three or four different courses; we went to the one that's right adjacent to the I-610 overpass. I went with my neighbor's young son, Collin Munster, who, I guess, was about twenty at the time. He was taking a course at Delgado on golf, and he was interested in playing. So, we drove over there, went to the clubhouse, paid the green fees, got a cart, and at that particular course, the course is not adjacent to the clubhouse, so we had to take the cart adjacent to the I-610 overpass and turn under the I-610 overpass. We loaded the clubs, drove down there, went under the underpass, and about maybe forty or fifty yards, we went to what is the little putting area, where you can practice your putts before you tee off. We parked the cart, we both got out, and within maybe a minute to a minute and a half of going under the overpass, we heard a bang. I turned around and saw the bus actually leaving the roadway, and it just skipped a couple of times, and it just crashed alongside the interstate on its side. It immediately started smoking, and I remember to this day, for a minute, it was like my eyes are deceiving me; I'm not really seeing this, because it was just so incredible, something you really didn't expect. Because the bus was smoking, someone said there must be a fire, so at that point, we all dropped what we were doing and ran; there were some other people over there. We went up like an embankment, which is on the side of the interstate. The bus was past the right railing on this embankment on its side, smoking, and other people got there about the time we did. It was a scene like a bomb went off. People were groaning and crying. Other people were outside the bus that had been thrown out the windows. It was like human carnage, and it was all elderly people. I'm not trained in any medical services or EMT, so it was a limit to what I can do. I don't recall if I climbed onto the bus; I think I was on the outside, trying to comfort people, trying to move them away from the bus. Of course, it's always dangerous to move anybody if you're not trained, so I just felt somewhat out of my element in trying to assist.*
>
> *When the medical personnel came, they needed help. Several of the people had IVs inserted, and one nurse or EMT had me hold the bag. Everyone in that bus was either killed or badly injured, I'm sure. Afterward, Collin*

and I went to a ceremony with the mayor, where they gave us a certificate for at least trying to assist people, so I still have that certificate somewhere.

New Orleans Mayor Marc Morial spoke of the heroes who came to assist at a press conference that was aired on CNN the afternoon of the crash: "The people, the motorists who stopped to assist are to be extremely commended. There were many, many good Samaritans on the road, who, when they saw what happened, didn't hesitate. They jumped out of their vehicles, and they went to work in an effort to try to save lives and assist."

Bergstrom continued:

What struck me also to this day is that had I stopped the cart for any reason, tie a shoelace, check on my clubs, we literally could have been under that I-610 as the bus came off the interstate, possibly hitting the golf cart. It left the roadway right before the path and then just hit the path because there was a gap there where the path is. It just kind of hit there and skipped and went further along the side of the interstate. Maybe a minute and a half, two minutes earlier, had I delayed us for any reason, that bus could've just crushed us.

An officer standing on the golf cart path, surveying the crash site. *Courtesy of* The Times-Picayune.

WWL and WDSU's Charles Zewe was working for CNN at the time and was live on the scene. Zewe reported from the I-610 overpass, overlooking the calamitous collision: "Motorists differ on what happened. The driver claims that he tried to avoid being cut off and suddenly swerved to the right, and he says he doesn't remember what happened after that, but motorists following along behind the bus tell a different story; they say the bus just suddenly, for no apparent reason, swerved out of control."

Eyewitness Margaret Messore was interviewed by Zewe and testified:

> *We were in our van, traveling about a quarter of a mile behind this bus, and a little car, the bus was in the left-hand lane, and the little car was about by his back quarter panel in the middle lane. The bus sort of swerved in on the little car but didn't hit it and swerved back into his lane. The little car slowed down, and the bus went from the left lane, all the way across into a cement metal embankment on the side of the road and just crashed full speed.*

The driver of the little green car remains a mystery today.

The 1997 Custom Bus Charters coach crashed at around 9:00 a.m., en route from LaPlace to Casino Magic in Bay St. Louis. Twenty-two of the forty-three passengers were killed, making this the worst vehicular accident in Louisiana history. All twenty-one survivors were injured, most of them seriously, including the driver, who died three months later of a heart attack while talking on the phone with a family member.

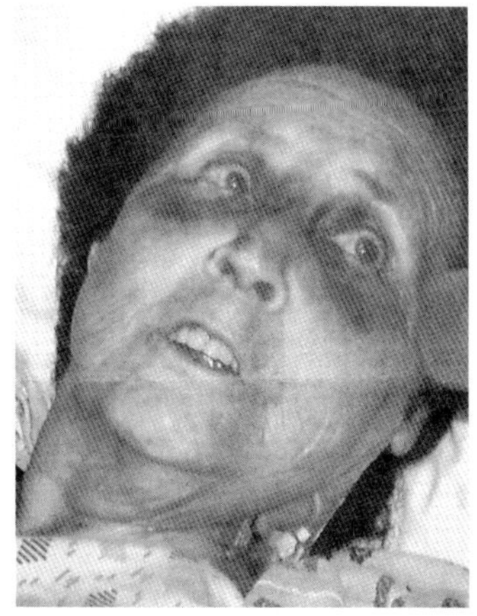

Survivor Anna Battard being interviewed at River Parishes Hospital, two days after the accident. *Courtesy of* L'Observateur.

Retired Sergeant Butch Remondet of the St. John Sheriff's Office lost his mother, Mildred, along with his aunt and several other relatives in the crash. Mildred was seventy years old. Inside his LSU-themed living room in Reserve, Remondet expressed his sentiments:

> *Going back to those days, of course, my mother was one of the greatest persons on earth. She did a lot of things for us. She loved to cook. She was always there to help us do different things. As life went on, she liked to go to the casinos and have good times. Whenever we*

> *could take her anywhere, we took her; we tried to do as many things with her after my father had passed away. She would hang around with us and do a lot of things with us.*

Mildred had been a widow for fourteen years. Love blossomed again when she met John Vicknair in 1997. Both had been together for nearly two years before the crash separated them forever. Remondet continued:

> *I begged her not to go on that trip. I bought her a guardian angel, bought her a card. I said, "Please stay here with us." She said she wanted to go with her friends. I just had a gut feeling. I really didn't want her to go. She said, "Well, I'm going." So, we decided to go to Tennessee. That day of the accident, we were barbecuing, and some of Linda's family came on running outside and said, "Your mother's on television; she got in a terrible bus wreck!" When I was looking at CNN, she was just laying there on the gurney, waving to everybody saying she was okay. So, I kind of hesitated about actually coming home, which I should've came home earlier, because I didn't make it home at the time she had passed away. It was tearing me up that I didn't leave when I should have left. Sometime that morning, my little brother called me up and said, "You can slow down and take your time, because she passed. They won't let you go in there and see her." It was hard, and that sticks in my mind a lot.*
>
> *She had bad legs and a lot of internal bleeding that we didn't know about. She passed away on the operating table. The doctor said she probably could've lived another ten to fifteen years if it wouldn't have been for this accident. Her heart was in good shape.*

Intensifying the agony, four families of the deceased reported large amounts of jewelry and cash were stolen from their loved ones. Mildred's locket she wore around her neck, along with $400 in cash she brought on the trip, were never recovered.

Lucien Gauff lost his mother, Shirley, in the accident. She was sixty-one years old. Lucien traced her life of servitude and recounted the day of the accident:

> *My mom was a schoolteacher, thirty-eight years my mom taught. She taught second grade, mostly at LaPlace Elementary. She initially started out at Woodland School and then eventually went to LaPlace Elementary and had been there for over thirty years. She loved to play bingo. She loved to*

Shirley Gauff. *Courtesy of Lucien Gauff III.*

hang out at the Place Dubourg, which was a retirement facility for senior citizens. So, she would go over there and volunteer and play bingo or go to casino trips; that was something she enjoyed doing. On that particular day, that was one the trips that she had planned for them. They had asked her to coordinate a Mother's Day bus trip.

They were going to Mississippi, and actually, my brother was coaching and teaching in Mississippi at the time. They were going to meet for lunch for Mother's Day. I was working for DuPont. I worked that night, and when I got off at 6:00 a.m., I went to my parents' house as I normally do, and when I got there, I saw the ice chest sitting on the carport. "Uh Oh! Mom's got a bus trip!" When I walked in, she said, "Yep, I'm going to the casino today!" She had already cooked food for me. "Tell your wife don't cook! She could come over and get food!" Everything was prepared. My mom was always looking for her treat. She'd say, "Awh, where's my treat?" which was money. It was Mother's Day, so I gave her money to go to the casino, or more money to have on her bus trip. Then I left and came back here [home], *and she called and said, "Don't forget, tell Allison to come and get the food, so you'll have food for later." "All right, Mom!" She left; I went to sleep, so I could be ready for work that night and eventually got a phone call, I guess about 10:30-something or 11:00, saying there had been an accident. It was one of my mom's friends. She was going to get on the bus at The Plaza in New Orleans East. "Lucien," she said, "there's been an accident. I'm not sure of the severity of it, but you need to call Charity Hospital and see what's going on, because they aren't telling us anything." I thought fender bender—that's what I'm thinking—so I got up and found the number, and while I was up, I turned on the TV. I'm talking to the lady at Charity and told her that I heard there was an accident. I was looking for Shirley Gauff, and the lady said, "Oh. OK. Fine, we got it. She's here; we have her." I got up to start getting dressed so that I could go to the hospital, and then an interruption on the TV came, "Breaking news—bus crashed in New Orleans. There's four fatalities and numerous people injured."*

"What? This isn't a fender bender; this is serious!" So, I hurried up, got dressed, made it out the door, called my dad to tell him, "Hey, Mom's bus has been in a crash!" He was working in Ponchatoula. "You need to meet me at the hospital." I made my way to Metairie, not thinking that this bus accident

was so bad that now the traffic was thick as thieves; it was backed up, bumper to bumper. "What in the devil's going on? Why can't I get through?" My cousin, who is a police officer here in St. John Parish, he was on his way to New Orleans because they told him his grandmother was on the bus. So, he flips on his lights, I got behind him, and we weaved our way through the traffic. When we got to the I-610 split, that's when I realized the highway's closed! That's why the traffic's backed up; they're not letting anybody through. When we got there, we stopped. He said, "Bo, I'm going to the scene of the accident." I said, "Well, I'm going to Charity. They told me my mom's at Charity." So, I continued, went into New Orleans, got to Charity, asked for my mom. They looked through a roll and said, "No, we don't have her." I said, "What do you mean you don't have her? When I called, you said you have her." They said, "No, there's a procedure that we go through when there's an accident, and especially with so many victims. So, what we're saying is, when we said, 'We have her,' we're putting her name on the role, because with an accident like that, purses are tossed, people don't have ID on them, we don't know who's on the bus, we don't know who's who. We don't know who's here. Can you walk through with me?" So, I got to go into every emergency room, every triage, every victim that came through, to try to identify my mom or identify any of the people that were on the bus. No, she's not here; she's not one of them. I waited around for a while, went back inside, asked them again, and still, no Shirley Gauff. And then someone at the hospital said, "Well, you may call the morgue; they may know." I called the morgue; the guy at the morgue was very nice and said, "No, no. We don't have anybody yet, but if I can be of any help, just let me know."

Lucien returned to the scene of the accident. His mother was not there either. Officials at the accident information post in City Park directed him back to Charity Hospital, thinking she's probably there. Lucien added:

On my way to Charity, I said, "Wait a minute; let me stop at the morgue." This has been hours now of looking for my mom. I pulled off on Tulane and Broad, went to the morgue, went in, and the guy that I talked to earlier called downstairs. The coroner came up, brought a bunch of pictures, and he took one picture out. He said, "Here you go, these are the ones we've processed so far. See if you could recognize any." I looked through a bunch of pictures, and I said, "No, none of them are familiar." He said, "OK, I have five more bodies downstairs; let me go process them, and I'll be back up." So, I waited about fifteen to twenty minutes, he came up, and this time, he didn't take the picture out, and he left that picture in. And as I was going through, when I got to that picture, I said, "That's my mom." He said, "Well, how can you tell?" And I said, "Because I saw her this morning, so I know what she was wearing." My mom had been decapitated, so that's why he asked how could I tell. So, he went downstairs, he grabbed her belongings, brought it up, and it was the diamond pendant I had given her, it was her wedding ring, it was the ring from my Aunt Yvonne, it was the gold bracelet that I had given her, so I said, "Yes, that's my mom."

Lucien then made the heartbreaking calls to his brother, Errol, who was at City Park awaiting news, and to his sister, Chermain, who was living in Dallas with her husband and was seven months pregnant. Lucien continued:

My mom had a bunch of ladies, they played PO-KE-NO, and she had gone to my brother's mother-in-law's house. They were playing PO-KE-NO, and it was right after the Columbine incident, and they were all talking. My mom told Murle, "I'm ready. This world is not the world that I remember and not the world I want to be in." It was about two weeks later when this [the bus crash] *happened.*

Resolute in her Catholic faith, Shirley's spiritual strength and service to others endure in her family today. Lucien recalled his mother's daily dedication to prayer, tears running down his face:

Every morning, before she would go to work, she would drive to New Orleans and go to St. Jude Novena and make it back. If she'd miss in the morning, she'd go in the evening. Still today, I have my St. Jude Novena book. It was one of those that we all made the Novena, because it was so special to her that we would all make time to go to the St. Jude Novena.

Service is what I need to do and where I need to be. I'm a Rotarian. I belong to the LaPlace Rotary Club so that I can give back, so that I can serve. On Monday nights, every two weeks, we go to Place Dubourg and play bingo with the seniors, and it is something that I do. I call bingo, or I go and facilitate bingo with those seniors. And just to see their faces, I know why she did it. I know why that was such a large part of what she did. And I would ask her, "Why do you spend so much time with those seniors?" And she would say, "Because when I get old, I want someone to spend time with me."

My sister's a teacher, my brother's a teacher, so they've all followed in my mom's footsteps: serving, teaching, influencing others.

St. James students recognized/6A

See Page 1C

L'OBSERVATEUR

"THE OBSERVER"

WEEKEND EDITION

Saturday, May 15, 1999

St. John Parish in mourning

Crash victims remembered; investigation continues

By LEONARD GRAY
L'Observateur

RESERVE – At the triple-funeral service Wednesday in St. Peter's Catholic Church, memories of Arto and Juanita Marse and Darnella Cambre filled the sanctuary.

Outside, LaPlace and Reserve fire department squads placed an archway of ladder trucks under which the three hearses passed on their way to the church's historic cemetery, while a double row of volunteer firefighters paid their respects.

It was yet another in the long procession of funerals which continued to numb the St. John the Baptist Parish community in the aftermath of the Mother's Day bus crash in New Orleans which killed 21 St. John Parish residents, mostly elderly.

Three white-draped caskets were set along the center aisle of St. Peter's Wednesday morning just after 10 a.m.

The Rev. Patrick Sanders comforted the capacity-filled church by quoting from the Gospel: "Do not let your hearts be troubled. You have faith in God, have faith in Me."

Arto "George" Marse Jr., 74, a former Reserve VFD chief, was remembered for his life of public service and his willing ministry, delivering flowers to patients at River Parishes Hospital from Chateau de Fleur while visiting friends.

"Most of what he enjoyed in life was serving his community," Sanders said.

In addition, his devotion to the Church was another telling point to his character.

Juanita "Nite" Marse, 73, was remembered as a tough disciplinarian to their children, as well as being honest and of high integrity, dedicated to the Rosary.

Darnella Cambre, 76, was likewise recalled

(See CRASH, Page 7A)

PASSING BENEATH an arc formed by the ladder trucks of the Reserve and LaPlace fire departments, honor is paid to Arto Marse and his wife, and to Darnella Cambre, whose husband, Jean, was also a Reserve firefighter before his death. Wednesday's funerals were only part of the aftermath of Sunday's tragic bus wreck which killed 22 persons. (Staff Photo by Leonard Gray)

Flowers Gauff helped students plant are reminder of beloved teacher

By DEBORAH CORRAO
L'Observateur

Last week the second-grade students in Shirley Gauff's class at LaPlace Elementary planted flowers outside their classroom window.

Monday morning those flowers served as remembrance of their well-loved teacher killed in Sunday's tragic bus accident.

LaPlace Elementary Principal Courtney Millet said the flowers are a perfect symbol of the 37-year veteran teacher's sunny personality.

Millet said Gauff always greeted everyone at the school with a cheerful "good morning" when she arrived at work.

"She was always so happy, always smiling," Millet said.

Millet said she was able to confirm the death of Gauff Sunday evening and worked with several teachers to contact all the teachers at LaPlace Elementary as well as the parents of Gauff's second-graders.

The next morning she met with all of the students in the second-grade center as soon as they arrived for class.

"One of Mrs. Gauff's students read an Amelia Bedelia book to the other second-graders," Millet said. "The children say Mrs. Gauff liked Amelia because she would laugh out loud when reading the books."

Later in the day, the children were

(See GAUFF, Page 5A)

SHIRLEY GAUFF
...Killed in bus crash

Sheriffs on alert after Columbine massacre

The front page of the River Parishes's *L'Observateur*, May 15, 1999. *Courtesy of* L'Observateur.

It was later revealed that the bus driver, Frank Bedell, had issues. Lucien responded like his mother would: "To say, 'Am I mad at him?' No. This was a man that was providing for his family, and I don't know what his situation was, so I couldn't be mad. It was just God's will."

Firefighter Elliott Sanders was there that terrible morning. From Fire Station 13 on Robert E. Lee Boulevard, the towering warrior spoke poignantly:

> *That day, I was an operator on the flying squad, which is a manpower and rescue unit. Sunday morning, we heard the call over the radio, and the captain at that time, Ricky Rocquin, he said, "Man, let's get in the truck!" When I pulled up to the scene, prior to anything else, we saw kind of what was there, and as the operator, I always try to use my fire truck to protect the firefighters, and I can direct traffic if I do it right. My choice that day was to just pull and block the interstate, once I looked over and saw what we had. The bus was sitting there, leaning at a degree. We were kind of*

concerned that it might roll all the way over. If I remember correctly, I know we did use some shoring to kind of hold it up, but not a lot. One of the main things I remembered was walking up and seeing what I thought was a wig laying at the front of the bus. Mr. Bedell, the driver, he was being taken away by a civilian; they put him in a car and took him away. He was still laying on the ground. Somebody scooped him up. Scoop and go basically, taking him to the hospital, and that wig, I later found out, was most likely a skullcap.

Patients, victims—whatever you want to call them—they were placed alongside the interstate, and they were laid down. We started administering first aid as best we could. Calls were being made for ambulances, assistance and so forth. At one point, I was standing there, and I had a small, portable oxygen tank—small, little green box—probably good for about twenty to thirty minutes max. I was giving oxygen to one patient who was laying there, and someone laid another patient right next to me. So, I'm looking at the oxygen and looking at the two patients now, and I couldn't decide which one, so I just started transferring the mask from one patient to the other, giving them both an opportunity and, hopefully, giving them a chance to survive until medical personnel got there and took over.

At one point, because of necessity, I was handing sand into the bus to help out, because the floors were literally covered in bodily fluids. You were slipping and sliding, so we decided to use sand, and when I was handing it in, before long, I found myself inside the bus with the guys. We carried those out that we could, and it turned into a more or less of a recovery mode. There were several people, one in particular that I remember at the front of the bus, who was basically wedged in, head facing forward, body more or less against the roof and legs downward. I'm quite sure that we used the Jaws of Life; we used several tools to actually remove those victims which we assumed had expired.

Disaster management? I think that's an oxymoron. You can't manage a disaster, nor can you fully plan for it. The equipment that we had—a bus involving forty-plus people? That's not something we trained and really thought about, so we came in, and we improvised to a big degree. The number of lives lost is always indelible, but we rarely mention the number of lives that we save.

The city of New Orleans, at any given time, does not have enough ambulances on the street staffed to handle a mass casualty, and this was a mass-casualty incident. The vehicles that were being used were civilians, just people that were on the interstate. They saw the accident, they pulled over and stopped to help. You know, that just goes to show you there is a lot of good, from that day, that people would actually pull over in a horrific scene, in their own personal vehicles, grab bloodied, mangled, injured people, put them in their vehicles and take them to the hospital. That is not something that we asked them to do; that's something that they decided to do on their own. We did not make any attempt to stop them. I don't know if we legally or rightfully could have. It happened. They took the people to the hospital, and hopefully, there were a lot of your survivors. In the midst of the chaos, firefighters, police, EMTs and regular citizens, they stepped up. We're not knights in shining armor; we're knights in dirty turnout gear, but we go out and we save lives, and that's what we did. That part of it kept get me going, knowing that we saved some lives.

Man, I would tell any firefighter starting today, I think the first class they ought to give in the academy should deal with some of the psychological things that you're going to encounter. There is no real way to prepare for it—but introduce it. There should be psychologists and psychiatrists on staff that the firefighters can easily reach out to and say, "Hey, man, just wait a minute. I need a little help." It takes strength to admit that you need help. I know. I didn't ask for long time, and I was being a coward because I didn't want to admit that, in my mind, I was suffering from some frailties. I

A *Times-Picayune* photograph of a fireman kneeling, examining the inside of the front of the bus. *Courtesy of* The Times-Picayune.

The bus crash site with firemen. *Courtesy of Chris Mickal.*

> *was doing the wrong things to try to counteract it; I was self-medicating—Johnnie Walker Black Label, Jose Cuervo after a while. I didn't do hard drugs, but I had quite a few drinks, and that's not the way to handle this. There's other methods that they have. I've been dealing with the veterans administration, who actually helped me with PTSD. It helped the city to recognize it. They have programs and, man, you got to ask.*

Multiple lawsuits followed the tragedy. Attorney Jerry Saporito represented the insurance company of Casino Magic in the case. From the Leake & Andersson Firm's Poydras Street boardroom, which overlooks the Crescent City skyline and bustling interstate traffic below, Saporito summarized the complex litigation that ensued:

> *The casino didn't have anything to do with selecting the tour operator, the bus company, the driver, the route. It really was, if you show up at the casino and spend the day with us, we're going to give you a brunch. It really wasn't a joint venture, but that's the way the plaintiffs and the families*

> *alleged the lawsuit in order to see if they can find another corporate-type defendant who would have a lot of insurance money to perhaps participate in some type of settlement.*

The date on which they were to gather at the federal court and meet with the magistrate to attempt to settle the case happened to be September 11, 2001. All of the plaintiff and defense attorneys gathered. Representatives of the insurance companies were available by telephone. Word had started to come in of the terrorist attacks at the World Trade Center in New York City; a lot of the people with the various insurance companies had perished in the attacks on the Twin Towers, so the magistrate agreed in the middle of the afternoon to shut down that day. The casino and bus manufacturer settled in federal court a few weeks after September 11. Saporito explained the intensive judicial management further:

> *The other litigation that grew out of this accident was in state district court here in New Orleans, and it was a litigation of, not all of the plaintiffs, but a lot of them, against the bus driver and the tour bus company, who, of course, was responsible for the actions of their driver, and it also was against the Louisiana Department of Transportation. The claim against Louisiana DOTD involved the guardrails. This accident, as you recall, happened on I-610 in the confines of City Park, and these guardrails, while they were designed to withstand an impact from a passenger car, they weren't certified to be able to withstand an impact from a big vehicle, like an eighteen-wheeler or a bus such as this one. The state judge, in a trial, no jury, ruled that the state highway department was 50 percent at fault because of the nature of these guardrails, and while they technically complied with the statute dealing with the guardrails that must be on the interstate highways, the judge found that it was reasonable for the state department of highways to know that these guardrails were not going to stop a big truck, a big bus like this. And if you recall, this particular location was within the confines of City Park and actually on the golf course, and there was a concrete underpass that ran under I-610, which allowed access to golfers in golf carts to get from one side of I-610 to the other side. That was an added danger that the judge found would have been an added reason for the state department of transportation to take additional steps, and it wasn't sufficient just to meet the minimum standard for these guardrails, but they should've done something more. It was foreseeable that it was a high risk of danger and a high risk of injury.*

A 2021 photograph of the site of the worst vehicular accident in Louisiana history. The area is abandoned and filled with graffiti. The author reached out to City Park's CEO in hopes of getting a memorial near the site on Zachary Taylor Drive, a haven for joggers and bikers. The request is being considered. (There is a memorial for the victims in front of the Place Dubourg in LaPlace.) *Author's collection.*

As of 2021, the guardrails pictured here at the crash site were built with the same construction requirements as those built in 1999. The federal law regarding guardrail safety was never advanced. *Author's collection.*

> *The other defendant in that case was the bus driver and the tour bus company. The judge found that they were 50 percent responsible as well. As the investigation was done on this particular bus driver, there was a lot of evidence that developed that perhaps he should not have been driving that bus. He had a couple of medical conditions involving his kidneys and his heart. He had been on kidney dialysis the day before. He testified to having trouble sleeping that entire night, and there was also some indication that he had used some type of medication or drugs that would impair his ability to drive.*
>
> *So, after hearing all of that evidence, the judge found that the driver and the bus company were at fault in actually causing the accident, and then the highway department was responsible for the other 50 percent for not having a guardrail that could help keep the bus on the highway.*

Federal safety requirements for bus drivers and manufacturers have improved since 1999. There were no seatbelts available for any of the passengers on the ill-fated bus. Today, seatbelts are required. Drivers today must undergo a medical qualification screening from a federally certified medical examiner before operating any commercial vehicle. Beginning in 2020, companies are required to annually check with a federal clearinghouse to ensure that current and prospective drivers do not have any alcohol or drug violations. All commercial drivers are now subject to random drug and alcohol testing. To prevent fatigued driving, companies today are required to equip their buses with electronic logging devices to record driver's compliance with federal limits on driving time.

During the production of this author's 2019 documentary, *Mother's Day Bus Crash on 610*, a bus of elderly passengers crashed en route from New Orleans to Harrah's Gulf Coast Casino in Biloxi. More than two dozen people were injured. The driver apparently had a medical issue and got drowsy.

BIBLIOGRAPHY

Anderson, Royd. *The Continental Grain Elevator Explosion*. Documentary film. New Orleans, LA: Lake Oaks Studio, 2007.

———. *The Luling Ferry Disaster*. Documentary film. Lafayette: University of Louisiana at Lafayette Department of Communication, 2006.

———. *Mother's Day Bus Crash on 610*. Documentary film. New Orleans, LA: Lake Oaks Studio, 2019.

———. *Pan Am Flight 759*. Documentary film. New Orleans, LA: Lake Oaks Studio, 2012.

———. *The UpStairs Lounge Fire*. Documentary film. New Orleans, LA: Lake Oaks Studio, 2013.

Atkinson, Paul. "Did Sniper Start Rault Fire?" *The Times-Picayune*, February 16, 1973, 1:4.

———. "Fire Marshal Says Fatal Rault Center Blaze Arson." *The Times-Picayune*, February 10, 1973, 1:6.

Ball, Millie. "Man Lifted Off Flaming Silo in Daring Helicopter Rescue." *The Times-Picayune*, December 23, 1977, 1:18.

Barbier, Sandra. "Saying Rosary Part of Prayers for World Peace." *The Times-Picayune*, October 20, 1985, F-1.

Belcher, Geoff. "Bus Crash On I-10: Multiple Agencies Respond After Dozens Injured." *The Sea Coast Echo*, March 16, 2019, 1:1.

Bouden, Barbara. "Fire Reveals Bias, Letter." *The Times-Picayune*, June 29, 1973.

Carr, Martha. "Panicked Families Await News." *The Times-Picayune*, May 10, 1999, A-1.

Chatelain, Kim. "Neighborhood Turned Upside Down by Crash." *The Times-Picayune/The States-Item*, July 12, 1982, 1:11.

Darby, Joe. "Dozier to Probe for Human Error." *The Times-Picayune*, December 23, 1977, 1:8.

Delery-Edwards, Clayton. *The UpStairs Lounge Arson: Thirty-Two Deaths in a New Orleans Gay Bar: June 24, 1973.* Jefferson, NC: McFarland, 2014.

DelGuzzi, Kristen. "Some Trapped in Mangled Wreck; Others Are Ejected." *The Times-Picayune*, May 10, 1999, A-1.

DuBos, Clancy. "Ferry Kept on Coming." *The Times-Picayune*, October 24, 1976, 1:1.

———. "29 Killed in Quarter Blaze—Blood, Moans: Charity Scene." *The Times-Picayune*, June 25, 1973, 1:1.

Fieseler, Robert W. *Tinderbox: The Untold Story of the UpStairs Lounge Fire and the Rise of Gay Liberation*. New York: Liveright Publishing Corporation, 2018.

Fire Prevention Division of the New Orleans Fire Department. "Investigation Report of Fire, Fire Report." L.W. Bergeron, June 24, 1973.

Griffin, Gareth. "Flames of Hate: The New Orleans UpStairs Lounge Fire, June 24, 1973." Master's thesis, University of Louisiana at Lafayette, 2008.

Hernon, Peter. *A Terrible Thunder: The Story of the New Orleans Sniper*. New York: Doubleday, 1978.

Katz, Allan. "New Charity Burn Unit Aids Fire Victims." *The States-Item*, June 27, 1973.

Laplace, John. "Scene of French Quarter Fire Is Called Dante's 'Inferno,' Hitler's Incinerator." *The Times-Picayune*, June 25, 1973, 1:1.

Lind, Angus. "15th Floor a Flaming Hell: 5 Who Jumped 'Had No Choice.'" *The States-Item*, November 30, 1972, 1:1.

———. "'If We Only Knew'—Vigil Continues for Some." *The States-Item*, October 21, 1976, A-9.

Lind, Angus, Lanny Thomas and Walt Philbin. "29 Dead in Quarter Holocaust—Fire Victims are Identified." *The States-Item*, June 25, 1973, 1:1.

Mullener, Elizabeth. "Rault Survivor Decided that Her Family Needed Her." *The Times-Picayune*, November 29, 1997, A-1.

New Orleans Department of Police. General Case Report, fire fatality, item no. F-21149-73. Detective Charles Schlosser and Detective Sam Gebbia, reporting officers; Lieutenant Edward O'Donnell, supervisor. August 30, 1973.

Nolan, Bruce. "Blast Death Toll Now 32; 4 Others Still Missing." *The Times-Picayune*, December 24, 1977, 1:1.

Philbin, Walt. "First the Horror—Then the Leap." *The States-Item*, June 25, 1973, 1:6.

Pope, John. "N.O. Bus-Crash Driver Dies of Heart Attack." *The Times-Picayune*, August 3, 1999, A-1.

Presley, Merikaye. "Minyard Contends Pilot Was Impaired." *The Times-Picayune*, October 30, 1976, 1:3.

———. "Ship Pilot: Ferries Commonly Give Way." *The Times-Picayune*, October 26, 1976, 1:1.

Rogers, Peter V., OMI. *Tragedy Is My Parish: Working for God in the Streets of New Orleans*. New Orleans: Habersham Corporation, 1983.

Segura, Chris. "Devastating French Quarter Fire Probed By 3 Agencies." *The Times-Picayune*, June 26, 1973, 1:1.

The States-Item. "Arson Suspected—Charred Rubble Sifted for Clues." June 26, 1973, 1:1.

———. "Blaze Victim No. 12 Positively Identified." June 28, 1973, 1:1.

———. "No Sprinklers but Rault Center Meets N.O. Safety Standards." December 1, 1972, 1:7.

Stekler, Paul Jeffrey, Kolker Andrew and Louis Alvarez. *Louisiana Boys: Raised on Politics*. Documentary film. N.p.: White Star, 1992.

Thomas, Lanny. "Air Bag for High-Level Jumps Given to Fire Department." *The States-Item*, June 4, 1974, A-6.

———. "2 Rooms from Rault Victims: Firemen Only Minutes Away?" *The States-Item*, December 1, 1972, 1:1.

The Times-Picayune. "Bar Suit Fire Is Charging 11." June 11, 1974.

———. "Blaze Victim Seeks Damages." June 21, 1974.

———. "Booze in Pilot House Bottle, FBI Reports." November 12, 1976, 1:19.

———. "Chief Feels Fire Arson." July 16, 1973, 1:1.

———. "Fatal Fire Probe Continues." June 28, 1973, 1:5.

———. "15 Killed in Grain Explosion: 10 Others Still Missing." December 23, 1977, 1:1.

———. "Fire Inspectors Count up 594 Violations of Codes." July 17, 1973.

———. "Ill-Fated Ferry Plied River for 50 Years." October 21, 1976, 1:5.

———. "Skipper New at Ferry Job." October 21, 1976, 1:1.

———. "13th Floor Fall Cause of Death." February 9, 1974, 1:6.

The Times-Picayune/The States-Item. "Crash Death Toll Is at 153 as Investigation Begins." July 11, 1982, 1:1.

———. "Pan Am Jet Slams into Kenner; More than 148 Are Feared Dead." July 10, 1982, 1:1.

Townsend, Johnny. *Let the Faggots Burn: The UpStairs Lounge Fire*. N.p.: BookLocker.com, 2011.

Treadway, Joan. "Copter Pilots Rescue Eight." *The Times-Picayune*, November 30, 1972, 1:1.

Wagner, Michael. "Victim's Rings Returned, Cash Missing, Son Says." *The Times-Picayune*, May 20, 1999, A-9.

Wardlaw, Jack. "Arson Probed in Killer Blaze; 4 Die in Rault Center Tragedy." *The States-Item*, November 30, 1972, 1:1.

———. "Follow Up: The Rault Fire." *The States-Item*, February 11, 1976, A-11.

Watrous, Laurence D., and NFPA staff. "High-Rise Fire in New Orleans." *Fire Journal*, May 1973.

ABOUT THE AUTHOR

Royd Anderson is a Cuban American filmmaker, teacher and historian from New Orleans. He specializes in Louisiana disasters that are usually not mentioned in Louisiana history textbooks.

Anderson produced many award-winning documentaries, such as *Pan Am Flight 759*, *The UpStairs Lounge Fire*, *The Continental Grain Elevator Explosion*, *Mother's Day Bus Crash on 610* and *The Luling Ferry Disaster.* His film on the ferry disaster served as his master's thesis project at the University of Louisiana at Lafayette. The success of this film led to the creation of a monument for the victims in 2009.

He has been an invited guest speaker at Princeton University, Tulane University, Loyola University New Orleans and the FBI New Orleans Division. Some of his TV appearances include spots on the Lifetime Movie Network, the National Geographic Channel, WYES's *Informed Sources* and WLAE's *Louisiana: The State We're In*.

Anderson received a Master of Science degree in Communication from the University of Louisiana at Lafayette, a Bachelor of Arts degree in English Literature from Loyola University New Orleans and an Associate degree in Science from Delgado Community College.

He can be reached at rcand@mygrad.loyno.edu